English Language Teaching Matters:

A Collection of Articles
and Teaching Materials

T0288505

English Language Teaching Matters:

A Collection of Articles
and Teaching Materials

Michael Berman, Mojca Belak
and Wayne Rimmer

BOOKS

Winchester, UK
Washington, USA

First published by O-Books, 2011
O-Books is an imprint of John Hunt Publishing Ltd., Laurel House, Station Approach,
Alresford, Hants, SO24 9JH, UK
office1@o-books.net
www.o-books.com

For distributor details and how to order please visit the 'Ordering' section on our website.

Text copyright: Michael Berman, Mojca Belak and Wayne Rimmer 2010

ISBN: 978 1 84694 411 6

A CIP catalogue record for this book is available from the British Library.

Design: Lee Nash

Printed in the UK by CPI Antony Rowe
Printed in the USA by Offset Paperback Mfrs, Inc

We operate a distinctive and ethical publishing philosophy in all
areas of our business, from our global network of authors to
production and worldwide distribution.

CONTENTS

Acknowledgements

"Away", the photo on the front cover, is of a painting by Maka Batiashvili, an artist from the Republic of Georgia. The photo of "The Gift" in the Chapter on Intrapersonal Intelligence is also by the same artist. To see more of her work, please visit www.maka.batiashvili.net

If any copyright holders have been inadvertently overlooked, and for those copyright holders that all possible efforts have been made to contact but without success, the author will be pleased to make the necessary arrangements at the first opportunity.

Introduction

Michael Berman has been teaching English as a Foreign language and giving talks and workshops at both National and International Conferences all through his working life, and this volume is a collection of the articles and materials he has written on the subject that have not been published in book form before. The Appendices were written by Dr Wayne Rimmer – the Director of Studies at International House in Moscow, and Mojca Belak – a lecturer at the University of Ljubljana in Slovenia, coordinator of the IATEFL Teacher Development Special Interest Group, and a trainer at Pilgrims in Canterbury.

As well as articles on particular approaches to language teaching, such as the application and use of NLP (Neuro-Linguistic Programming), Howard Gardner's Multiple Intelligences Theory, and William Glasser's Choice Theory, you will also find plenty of practical teaching materials to make use of with your students – first day activities, for example, stories with suggestions for follow-up work, lead-ins to introduce new topics, and grammar exercises too.

***

All the materials presented in this volume and the suggestions as to how to use them, are based on the principles set out below, principles that can serve to guide us in how to be effective in our roles:

- The importance of providing learners with choice, instead of using the same approach with everyone, being sensitive to the fact that we are all unique, each with a different mix of Intelligence Types and Learning Styles, and each coming into the classroom with different personal histories that affect our attitude towards what we do and learn there.

- The fact that there is nothing wrong with Teacher Talking Time as long as it is used productively. After all, why do the majority of students come to us? Because they want the opportunity to be exposed to good models of English, which they might lack in the places they have come to us from.

- That humour is sacred as it helps to create an atmosphere in which students can feel relaxed and so produce their best work – where learning can flourish and where mistakes are seen for what they are – steps in the learning process that enable us to achieve our goals.

- The fact that the more we are able as teachers to hold ourselves back and avoid the temptation to intervene in order to offer a helping hand, the more the learners show themselves to be capable of. For we must never lose sight of our main goal, which is to empower rather than dis-empower those we work with.

- That 'the main purpose of higher education is to facilitate and expand students' understanding', (Ramsden, 2003, p. 8). And if we agree that learning methods 'must reflect real social practices' (Chanier, 2000, p. 83), then we have to conclude that learning must be anchored into 'real-world or authentic contexts that make learning meaningful and purposeful' (Bonk and Cunningham 1998, p. 27).

References

Bonk C.J., & Cunningham, D. (1998). Searching for learner-centered, constructivist, and sociocultural components of collaborative educational learning tools. In C. J. Bonk & K. King (Eds.), *Electronic collaborators: Learner-centered technologies for literacy, apprenticeship, and discourse* (pp. 25–50). Mahwah: Lawrence Erlbaum Associates.

Chanier, T. (2000). Hypermédia, interaction et apprentissage dans des systèmes d'information et de communication: Résultats et agenda de recherche. In L. Duquette & M. Laurier, (Eds.), *Apprendre une langue dans un environnement multimédia* (pp. 179–210). Outremont: Les Editions Logiques.

Ramsden, P. (2003). *Learning to teach in higher education.* London: Rutledge Falmer.

I

The Calling: A Form of Pilgrimage

I shall be telling this with a sigh
Somewhere ages and ages hence:
Two roads diverged in a wood, and I –
I took the one less traveled by,
And that has made all the difference.

From "Road Not Taken" by Robert Frost

Something drew me to the announcement of a Conference for English Language teachers to be held in Georgia although, to be entirely honest, at that stage I did not even know where it was. I just felt that I had to go there so I immediately sent details of the presentations I could offer to the contact person, and then promptly forgot all about it. However, some time later I received a reply. The answer was yes, they would be delighted to have me and to arrange accommodation as long as I could cover the cost of the fare. That was easily arranged as the College where I worked was prepared to do that. But the next problem was how to get to the venue as there were no flights to Georgia from the UK at that time.

It seemed I had to fly to Frankfurt, and then take an Air Georgia plane to Tbilisi, the ticket for which could only be purchased at the Air Georgia desk in Frankfurt airport. I arrived expecting to pay by credit card but only American dollars were acceptable so I then had to find a cash point machine, withdraw the money in marks and convert it at a Bureau De Change. To make matters worse, there followed a five-hour delay on the runway. Apparently the airport fees hadn't been paid by the impoverished airline so the pilot wasn't given clearance for take-off until the bill was finally settled with the dollars my fellow travellers and I had handed over at the desk.

The reason why there were no flights from the UK as I found out later was that the planes, all Aeroflot rejects, were not deemed to be airworthy. Hardly surprising when you consider that half of the seats had no seatbelts and the toilet did not even have a door that closed. My main concern, however, was that as the plane was making its final descent into Tbilisi, the one and only pilot had joined the passengers and was drinking wine and singing with them in the aisle. Who, if anybody, was in the cockpit I'll never know, but amazingly we landed safely.

Most places you visit can be compared to somewhere else you've been but Georgia was truly an exception. There's no way it can be neatly classified and categorised and that's part of its attraction. The people had hardly anything, recovering as they were from the after-effects of their struggle for independence and a civil war, but whatever they did have they would share with you. Fiercely independent, they would never admit to the difficulties they were experiencing and acted as if everything was just fine.

Life revolved around the extended family, without whose support nobody could have survived through those times. The only form of social activity was sitting round the table for extended feasts to which everyone who came contributed something. A Tamada would be appointed, always a man, and he would make an endless series of toasts for which we were all obliged to stand and drink. This was done from a Khanzi, a hollowed-out horn, so the wine, all locally produced, had to be drunk in one swig, as the horn, once drained of its contents, could only be laid on its side. Candles were always placed on the table, not for any decorative purpose but in preparation for the inevitable electricity cuts that would occur without any warning.

As for the Conference itself, despite the fact that there was no electricity and no equipment, not to mention the fact that I had to give my sessions by candlelight wrapped up in a coat, the enthusiasm of the delegates, starved for so long of contact with native speakers of English, was truly contagious. And despite the fact that there were no textbooks in the schools, ridiculously overcrowded classes and antiquated methods, the standard of English was remarkably high.

One Professor at the State University, an elderly woman, stood out from all the rest. She was always accompanied by one of her students with whom she would walk arm in arm. I later found out that this was because she had been blind since birth. Despite the fact that Braille was unheard of in Georgia, her English was native speaker level. She had a photographic memory and her students read to her and escorted her in return for lessons. Her fighting spirit and ruthless determination to succeed despite all the odds won my wholehearted admiration. No doubt she was an impossible person to live with, being extremely tyrannical and selfish, but nobody could fail to admire her resolve, which represented everything the younger Georgians had lost. For a generation the State had provided for them, so they had no need to do anything for themselves. Now that the situation was reversed they were totally lost. They had no idea how to use their new power to take control of their lives and just regarded themselves as victims of circumstance. This coupled with the revival of the Nationalist movement with the resultant disinterest in alliances with other states (surely the only way forward for such a small country) left a fertile land inhabited by people with a rich culture with an extremely bleak outlook.

Anyway, I'm starting to digress and it's time I returned to the subject. At the end of the Conference there was a farewell dinner in the organiser's house to which Ketevan had been invited. She brought her guitar along and sung an old Beatles' song, I believe it was "Yesterday" while another of the teachers accompanied her. At the first available opportunity I went over to her and tried to make conversation. But my introduction was followed by silence on her part. Then she blurted out "I've got two children" I didn't know how to respond. "Really? Tell me about them." I'd actually noticed her earlier when she walked through the Conference Hall, arriving late for one of my sessions. I'd also observed that she sat through the repeat. I vainly thought this was because she'd enjoyed it so much although it turned out that she was simply too tired to move on to the other hall and used the session to have a little nap in. And that's how it all started. It was the ultimate challenge and I couldn't resist it. It turned out I was the first foreigner Ketevan had ever spoken to, so her suspicion and mistrust were understandable.

I managed to persuade her to go out for dinner with me the following night, the last night before my return. My presentations over, I felt more relaxed and showed her my better side. And yes it was love at first sight. I kissed her good night outside my hotel, not expecting to see her again. But the next morning I found her waiting at the airport, which is when I invited to come to London for a holiday. The holiday turned into a happy ever after and we remain together to this day.

I would be lying if I said it has been plain sailing as the culture shock that hit Kate when she first arrived was immense. And I was not as patient as I might have been, not used to having to deal with someone else's problems in addition to my own. Not being assertive by nature, it took Kate a long time to find any work and it was a struggle for me to support us both and pay all the household bills too. However, we have slowly and painfully adapted to our new roles and hopefully the worst is now behind us. Irakli and Natia, Kate's children, live with their grandparents but come to join us for their long summer holidays each year. And now we're trying to have a child of our own.

Do I have any regrets? - None at all. Moreover, despite all the temptations due to the nature of my work, I have stayed faithful, something I have never succeeded in doing before. And am I

7

happy? That's a question I have never been able to answer, possibly as I still have to learn to love myself and happiness can truly only stem from that. But that's another story!

***

Whan that Aprille with his shoures sote
The Droghte of Marche
Hath perced to the rote...
Than longen folk to goon on pilgrimages

From "The Canterbury Tales" by Chaucer

An instinctive longing to move with the seasons has been with us since before we were 'human'. The call to Pilgrimage can be as profound as such an instinct. When we are called to go on Pilgrimage we enter into a special relationship with landscape, time and place that hallows both Way and Wayfarer in a way that that can only be understood through personal experience.

A pilgrimage can deepen our relationship with place and is also profoundly balancing and grounding, no doubt that is why so many are called to it after experiencing a life change, loss of a loved one, or a spiritual experience. The calling can take many forms. A longing, a desire to learn about a deity associated with a particular place, synchronicities that all point at the same desti-nation, or just a slow growing idea that takes shape over months or even years. The important thing is our response. In a sense, preparing for a long pilgrimage involves letting go of a previous self (often in a very real way, leaving jobs, homes, family and security be behind) and making room for a new self to emerge. (An extract from the article "Pilgrimage for Pagans" by Kate Fletcher & Corwen ap Broch. In *Pagan Dawn*, Beltane 2009).

Although I did not fully realize it at the time, my first visit to Georgia turned out to be very much a pilgrimage and the start of a new life, in the same way as our overseas students' first study trip to an English-speaking country often turns out to be. In other words, it is frequently a highly significant period in their lives in which their main preoccupations have little if anything to do with learning English. In fact, as a form of pilgrimage, such a journey can even take the form of an initiatory process:

Although its outer forms may sometimes appear to be different, the initiatory process has common features in all religions and spiritual traditions. In Buddhist tradition, the journey of the Buddha towards enlightenment combines worldly renunciation and austerity with the use of meditative techniques to quiet the overactive mind, cultivating detachment and inner peace; significantly, the Buddha's inner journey is also connected with a profound reconnection with the natural world. He leaves, the city and enters the forest, where he teaches the deer and finally finds enlightenment under a bodhi tree, assisted by a serpent deity called the Naga King as well as by the Earth Mother. In Christian tradition, the equivalent initiatory path is represented most clearly by the discipline and unworldliness of the monastic life, which began in the early Christian era with monks moving to live in the desert between Egypt and Palestine. Christian mystical tradition sees a 'dark night of the soul' as central to the process of inner purification, and often compares the soul's initiatory journey to stages in the life of Jesus Christ, culminating in his crucifixion and resurrection. Here, as in several other mystical traditions, including forms of Hindu asceticism and Buddhist tantra, the individual's meditation upon suffering, death and impermanence of the flesh is a vital stage in the initiatory process. In Celtic myth and in the Grail legends that it shaped, a commitment to the initiatory journey is often represented by the crossing of one or more 'perilous bridges'. These dangerous crossings are the testing gateways to the Grail castle, where deeper spiritual insights may be obtained. (An extract from Mann, N. & Glasson, P., 2009, 'The Glastonbury Experience & the Path of Initiation' In AVALON, Issue 42, summer 2009).

Being English Language teachers, whether we like it or not is actually a very small part of our jobs, and if we pretend otherwise then our effectiveness to help those who are entrusted to us is clearly greatly diminished.

PS. To bring the above story up to date, nearly fifteen years have passed since my first visit to Georgia described above. It turned out that we were unable to have children of our own, but Natia and Irakli both moved to the UK to live here with us. As for Ketevan, she is now the Managing Director of Caucasus Arts, a company set up to promote both visual and performing artists from Georgia, Armenia, Azerbaijan, and the other independent states in the region. And *Georgia through Its Folktales*, with tales translated by Ketevan and notes on them written by me, was published in paperback by O-Books in March 2010.

Journeys bring power and love
back into you.
If you cannot go somewhere
move in the passages of the self.
They are like shafts of light,
always changing,
and you change
when you explore them

Jelaluddin Rumi – 13th century Sufi

2

Your First Day with a New Class

Is this new teacher any good? – The students wonder. *Are they going to like me?* – You ask yourself. What do you do first day with a new class? Clearly this will depend on their level and whether they already know each other or not. However, we each have our preferred activities and here is something I frequently use with classes from Intermediate level upwards – first day questionnaires. Four different sets of questions are used to ensure a variety of different answers result and to prevent the listeners from getting bored with what they hear during the reporting back stage.

While listening to the reports, I make notes in two columns, on a sheet of paper or an OHT, of the effective language used and also of the problems that reveal themselves. At the end of the lesson, so as not to interrupt the flow during the productive stage, I then go through these together with the class as a whole. First of all, I focus on the effective language that was produced to provide the learners with positive "strokes", and then point out the errors, asking them to self-correct if possible and to explain why the utterances were problematic. Obviously this has to be done selectively, just focussing on those points you consider to be the most important to deal with, taking the students' needs and level into account, so as not to undermine their self-confidence in their ability to get their messages across. The last thing you want to do is to inhibit the learners from practising their English, which is why it is important not to overdo the error correction. The aim is to promote fluency, but not at the expense of accuracy.

What I particularly like about this lesson is that first of all it is relatively easy to set up, secondly that it provides for plenty of STT, and thirdly that the feedback stage is an opportunity for you to show the class that you know your stuff (through your grammar explanations). In this way you can gain the learners' respect right from the start, an essential prerequisite to ensuring their cooperation and a successful working relationship for the duration of the course.

FIRST DAY QUESTIONNAIRE (SET A): Work in pairs. Choose five questions from the list below to ask your partner. Your partner will then do the same and ask you five questions. Both of you should make a note of the answers you get as you will then be asked to tell the rest of the class the most interesting things you found out about each other:

- What's the most beautiful landmark in your hometown and what's the ugliest?
- What do you miss most when you're away from home?
- What's the best way of overcoming depression?
- If you could be invisible for a day, where would you go and what would you do?
- When was the last time you broke the law?
- When and where were you happiest?
- When did you last lose something valuable and what was it?
- What last made you cry?
- If your house was on fire, which three things would you try to rescue first?
- What is your pet hate?

FIRST DAY QUESTIONNAIRE (SET B): Work in pairs. Choose five questions from the list below to ask your partner. Your partner will then do the same and ask you five questions. Both of you should make a note of the answers you get as you will then be asked to tell the rest of the class the most interesting things you found out about each other:

- Where is home for you?
- And what would you advise a tourist visiting your home town to see or do?
- What animal would you most like to be?
- If you could be Mayor for the day, what would you like to do?
- What are your guilty pleasures?
- What would you like written on your tombstone?
- If you could live anywhere you wanted to, where would you chose and why?
- What makes you laugh?
- What makes you cry?
- What cause, if any, would you be prepared to die for?

FIRST DAY QUESTIONNAIRE (SET C): Work in pairs. Choose five questions from the list below to ask your partner. Your partner will then do the same and ask you five questions. Both of you should make a note of the answers you get as you will then be asked to tell the rest of the class the most interesting things you found out about each other:

- What single thing would most improve the quality of your life?
- What is your greatest regret?
- What are you reading at present?
- When and where were you happiest?
- Who are your favourite musicians?
- Who or what is the greatest love of your life?
- What is the trait you most deplore in others?
- If you could buy anything you wanted, what would you chose?
- Where would you love to go on holiday and why?

- Which living person do you most despise?

FIRST DAY QUESTIONNAIRE (SET D): Work in pairs. Choose five questions from the list below to ask your partner. Your partner will then do the same and ask you five questions. Both of you should make a note of the answers you get as you will then be asked to tell the rest of the class the most interesting things you found out about each other:

- What is your idea of perfect happiness?
- Which living person do you most admire and why?
- Which trait do you most deplore in yourself?
- On what occasions do you lie?
- What objects do you always carry with you?
- Who are your favourite writers?
- Which talent would you most like to have?
- What is your greatest fear?
- How would you like to be remembered?
- What is your greatest extravagance?

The two sets of questions that follow can be used the same way but were produced for a class of Business English students:

FIRST DAY QUESTIONNAIRE (Set i): Choose three of the following questions to ask the person sitting next to you. Make a note of their answers so you can report back your findings to the rest of the class:

- Tell me about a city or a country you have visited in connection with your job.
- What are three of the most important things you do in your job?
- What's the biggest challenge your company or institution faces in the future?

- What are the three most essential qualities of a person who does your job well?
- Tell me about a book or an article that you have read which has really influenced you in your work.
- Tell me about a personal achievement connected with your work that you are particularly proud of.
- What job would you like to have if you didn't have your present job?

FIRST DAY QUESTIONNAIRE (Set ii): Choose three of the following questions to ask the person sitting next to you. Make a note of their answers so you can report back your findings to the rest of the class:

- Tell me three things that would irritate you in a colleague.
- What are you most looking forward to in your job in the weeks or months ahead?
- Tell me about a personal achievement in your job that you are particularly proud of?
- Tell me about someone you really admire in your field, or someone you really admire because of the work they have done.
- What's the most challenging or difficult aspect of your job?
- Tell me about three ambitions you have.
- What job would you like to have if you didn't have your present job?

***

The activity that follows is one that can be used by trainers on the first day of an Overseas Teachers Course. Ask the participants, while mingling, to find someone who has an interesting story to tell about something that happened to them in one of the following situations:

- On a plane, a train or a boat
- At work
- At a doctor's surgery or in a hospital
- In a hotel
- While shopping
- In a classroom
- While sightseeing
- In a cinema or a theatre
- While giving some kind of public performance
- In a bank or a post office
- While waiting in a queue
- In a park
- In a museum or an art gallery
- At an interview for a job
- In a nightclub, a bar, or a pub
- In a temple, a church, or any other holy place
- At a party
- In a library or a police station
- In a restaurant
- On a horse, a camel, an elephant, or a ladder

The participants can then take it in turns to report back to the class as a whole about the most interesting thing they found out. Alternatively, if you have the opportunity to get to know the members of the group on an individual basis before the start of the course, their backgrounds and their hobbies, you can person-alise this *Find Someone Who* activity with questions like the following examples:

Find someone who

- Practises Yoga
- Has taught in a prison
- Plays the saxophone in a jazz band

- Has been invited to Buckingham Palace
- Used to be a professional footballer

***

A variation on the "I went to market" game

If you are unfamiliar with the game, this is how it is usually played:

A: I went to market and I bought a kilo of potatoes.

B: I went to market and I bought a kilo of potatoes and a bunch of bananas.

C: I went to market and I bought a kilo of potatoes, a bunch of bananas, and a tin of baked beans.

And this is how it can be adapted for use on the first day with a new class:

A: My names Michael and I've got no hair.

B: Your names Michael and you've got no hair. My name's _____ and I've got _____

Who am I?

Ask each learner to pick a number between one and fifty, and to keep that number secret. Then show the list below on an overhead transparency, interactive whiteboard, or as part of a power point presentation. Each learner is required to take on the identity of the person whose number they have chosen and, working in pairs, the students discover each other's identity by

playing 20 Questions – with all the questions being of the YES/
NO variety. For example, "Are you alive?" or "Were you a
writer?" rather than "What is your occupation?"

To avoid making this too much of a General Knowledge test,
if anyone is not familiar with the person whose number they
select, invite them to choose one number higher or lower
instead. Additionally, you could change the names of the famous
people in the list, to ensure the class members will be familiar
with all of them.

1 Pablo Picasso 2 Christopher Columbus 3 Queen Victoria 4
Nelson Mandela 5 J.S. Bach 6 Cleopatra 7 Karl Marx 8 Marco
Polo 9 Margaret Thatcher 10 William Shakespeare 11 Van Gogh
12 Marilyn Monroe 13 W.A. Mozart 14 Napoleon Bonaparte 15
Madonna 16 Igor Stravinsky 17 Henry VIII 18 Jane Austen 19
Michelangelo 20 Michael Jackson 21 Emily Bronte 22 Albert
Einstein 23 Carl Jung 24 Diana, Princess of Wales 25 Julius
Caesar 26 Salvador Dali 27 Mother Theresa 28 Nostradamus 29
Leo Tolstoy 30 Eva Peron 31 Leonardo da Vinci 32 Bob Dylan 33
Saint Joan of Arc 34 Paul McCartney 35 Paolo Coelho 36 J.K.
Rowling 37 Isaac Newton 38 Josef Stalin 39 Catherine the Great
40 Abraham Lincoln 41 Vasco da Gama 42 Florence Nightingale
43 Geoffrey Chaucer 44 Mohamed Ali 45 Anne Frank 46 Roger
Federer 47 Joseph Conrad 48 Marie Curie 49 Frederic Chopin 50
David Beckham

***

In common

This is a first day activity that can be used with learners at any
level, from Elementary to Advanced, which requires the use of no
equipment or hand-outs. Invite the learners to work in pairs,
ideally with someone they do not already know, and to find three
things they have in common and three things they do not have in

common with each other. They can then report back to the rest of the class, like the two students do in the following example:

Student A: I spoke to Yoko and I found out that we both enjoy watching soaps on TV

Student B: I spoke to Giorgi and I found out that unlike me he's a vegetarian.

**

My hopes for the course

I hope that by the end of this course I will be able to feel I've done a good job and that I did not let you or myself down in any way. And I hope you will feel you have learnt something useful that will enable you to be more effective teachers, and that you will feel renewed enthusiasm for the jobs you do.

Tell the learners about your hopes for the course, like the example above, then in small groups have them write down at least three things that they hope to get from it. Then invite them to share what they have come up with. To follow this up, also in the groups, have them come up with three questions they would like to ask you, and then let them ask them.

**

Spot the lie

I have a tattoo of a frog on my left forearm.
I've been married three times.
I have no children.
I never drink milk and I'm a teetotaller.

Write four facts about yourself on the board or on an overhead transparency, like the examples above. Three of the facts are true, and one is false. Ask the learners to guess which one, and the reason for the choice they make. This gives you the chance to tell them a little about yourself. Then, get each student to write four statements about themselves. Three statements are true, while one is false. Invite each student to read their four statements to the class and the rest of the class to guess which statement isn't true.

The Answers:
> *I have a tattoo of a frog on my left forearm. (False - it's on my right forearm).*
> *I've been married three times. (True – but hopefully I've learnt from my mistakes!).*
> *I have no children. (True, but I do have two stepchildren).*
> *I never drink milk and I'm a teetotaller. (True).*

***

Finally, I would like to share an alternative first day activity with you that is suitable for use with Intermediate, Upper Intermediate, and Advanced classes. It works particularly well with Intrapersonal Intelligence types (those learners who prefer to have the chance to look within before sharing their views). This is because it gives them the opportunity to work on their own before being required to work with a partner, and this makes them more receptive to working in pairs when the time for it comes.

Set A: Work individually and complete five of the following sentence starters. Then find a partner and tell him or her all about yourself. Finally, report back to the rest of the class the most interesting facts you found out about each other.

If I could change one thing about myself, I would _____

The most romantic thing anyone has ever done for me is _____

If I can I always try to avoid _____

To wake myself up in the morning _____

Last thing at night I always _____

If I have time to myself _____

When I'm feeling down _____

My happy place is _____

My best friend is _____

You may not know it but I'm no good at _____

Set B: Work individually and complete five of the following sentence starters. Then find a partner and tell him or her all about yourself. Finally, report back to the rest of the class the most interesting facts you found out about each other.

Not a lot of people know this but I'm very good at _____

It's not good for my image, but I have to admit I like _____

My biggest influence is _____

If I could pass any law, I'd _____

The song or piece of music I can never get out of my head is

_____

When I was a child I wanted to be _____

My biggest regret is _____

The shop I can't walk past is _____

I know I'm having "a bad hair day" when _____

My last meal would be _____

3

Tales of Power

The stories featured in this chapter are all examples of what Jürgen Kremer, transpersonal psychologist and spiritual practitioner, called "tales of power" after one of Carlos Castaneda's novels. He defines such texts as conscious verbal constructions based on numinous experiences in non-ordinary reality, "which guide individuals and help them to integrate the spiritual, mythical, or archetypal aspects of their internal and external experience in unique, meaningful, and fulfilling ways" (Kremer, 1988, p.192). In other words, they can serve the purpose of not only helping learners to develop their language skills, but also, and more importantly, they can also be used for facilitating personal development.

Before presenting the tales, for those of you who might be new to storytelling, and who might be feeling apprehensive about telling one in class for the first time, here are some introductory tips:

- Make an outline of the story using your own words or produce a mind map.

- Practise telling the story in front of a mirror or to a friend.

- Remember that storytelling is a task shared by the teller and the listener.

- Tell rather than read the story, is possible.

- Accept that making mistakes is a natural part of storytelling.

- The nervousness you feel beforehand is your performance energy. Remember that your emotions are under your control.

- Last, but certainly not least, if you make sure you enjoy the experience, nine times out of ten your learners will too!

The Three Wishes

Once upon a time there was a widow who had heard that God would undoubtedly fulfil three wishes wished by anyone on the fifteenth night of the fast of Ramadan. The good woman got quite impatient: "Oh, if it were only Ramadan already!"

Who knows whether she had long to wait? At any rate Ramadan came at last, and then very soon the fifteenth night of the fast. At midnight the widow uttered her first wish: "Oh God, make my son's head bigger!" Her wish was fulfilled at once: in one moment her son's head had become as big as an iron kettle. The widow could hardly believe her eyes, but it was so. Terrified, she uttered her second wish: "Lord! Make my son's head smaller!" And his head grew less and less till it was hardly as big as a millet seed! But now the good woman came to her senses and uttered her third wish: "Almighty God! Make my son's head again as it was before!"

And this wish too was fulfilled to her.

Notes for teachers

Ask the learners to imagine they could have three wishes granted, any three things that they wanted. What would they choose, and why? Invite them to get together in small groups to compare their answers. You can then read or tell them the above story, which is about what happened to a poor widow in Daghestan who had just such an opportunity. It is an Avar tale taken from Adolf Dirr's 1925 collection, *Caucasian Folk-tales*, translated into English by Lucy Menzies and published in London by J.M. Dent & Sons Ltd. The Avars, a Lesghian race, are based in present-day Daghestan in the Caucasus.

Heaven Can't Wait!

Two ninety year old men, Mike and Joe, have been friends all their lives.

When it's clear that Joe is dying, Mike visits him every day. One day Mike says, 'Joe, we both loved rugby all our lives, and we played rugby on Saturdays together for so many years. Please do me one favour, when you get to Heaven, somehow you let me know if there's rugby there.'

Joe looks up at Mike from his death bed, 'Mike, you've been my best friend for many years. If it's at all possible, I'll do this favour for you.'

Shortly after that, Joe passes on. At midnight a couple of nights later, Mike is awakened from a sound sleep by a blinding flash of white light and a voice calling out to him, 'Mike-Mike.'

'Who is it? Asks Mike sitting up suddenly. 'Who is it?'

'Mike - It's me, Joe.'

'You're not Joe. Joe just died.'

'I'm telling you, it's me, Joe,' insists the voice.

'Joe! Where are you?'

'In heaven', replies Joe. 'I have some really good news and a little bad news.'

'Tell me the good news first,' says Mike.

'The good news,' Joe says, 'is that there is rugby in heaven. Better yet, all of our old friends who died before us are here, too. Better than that, we're all young again. Better still, it's always spring time and it never rains or snows. And best of all, we can play rugby all we want, and we never get tired.'

'That's fantastic,' says Mike. 'It's beyond my wildest dreams! So what's the bad news?'

'You're in the team for Tuesday!'

***

If there's a heaven, what would you like to do there that you can do here?

Think about what you wouldn't miss from this life in heaven, and make a list of all the things that annoy you here every day. (Perhaps you wouldn't miss getting up early in the mornings or doing homework, for example).

Now, without looking back at the text, place all the parts of the story in the correct order:

a. 'Better still, it's always spring time and it never rains or snows. And best of all, we can play rugby all we want, and we never get tired.'

b. 'I'm telling you, it's me, Joe,' insists the voice.

c. 'In heaven', replies Joe. 'I have some really good news and a little bad news.'

d. Joe looks up at Mike from his death bed, 'Mike, you've been my best friend for many years. If it's at all possible, I'll do this favour for you.'

e. 'Joe! Where are you?'

f. 'Mike - it's me, Joe.'

g. Shortly after that, Joe passes on. At midnight a couple of nights later, Mike is awakened from a sound sleep by a blinding flash of white light and a voice calling out to him, 'Mike-Mike.'

h. 'Tell me the good news first,' says Mike.

i. 'That's fantastic,' says Mike. 'It's beyond my wildest dreams! So what's the bad news?'

j. 'The good news,' Joe says, 'is that there is rugby in heaven. Better yet, all of our old friends who died before us are here, too. Better than that, we're all young again.

k. Two ninety year old men, Mike and Joe, have been friends all their lives.

l. When it's clear that Joe is dying, Mike visits him every day. One day Mike says, 'Joe, we both loved rugby all our lives, and we played rugby on Saturdays together for so many years. Please do me one favour, when you get to Heaven, somehow you let me know if there's rugby there.'

m. 'Who is it? Asks Mike sitting up suddenly. 'Who is it?'

n. 'You're in the team for Tuesday!'

o. 'You're not Joe. Joe just died.'

1 ___ 2 ___ 3 ___ 4 ___ 5 ___ 6 ___ 7 ___ 8 ___ 9 ___ 10 ___ 11 ___
12 ___ 13 ___ 14 ___ 15 ___

ANSWERS: 1-k / 2-l / 3-d / 4-g / 5-m / 6-f / 7-o / 8-b / 9-e / 10-c /
11-h / 12-j / 13-a / 14-i / 15-n

The Cracked Pot

Level: Intermediate - Upper Intermediate
Target Audience: Adults
Language / Skills Focus: Listening & Speaking
Materials: Photocopies of the worksheet. Photocopies of the story
(optional) to hand out at the end of the session. A drawing on the
board or an OHT of a cup that's half-full or half-empty.

IN CLASS

1. *Pre-listening*: What do you see when you look at the
   drawing - a cup that's half full or a cup that's half empty?
   And what does this say about the kind of person you are?
   Now listen to the story.

2. *While-listening*: Pause after the line 'As we return to the
   Master's house, I want you to notice the beautiful flowers
   along the path' and ask the learners why the water carrier
   said this to the pot. They can then listen to the rest of the
   story to see whether their answers were correct or not.

3. *Post-listening*: Now that you've listened to the story, look at
   the drawing of the cup again. What do you see this time? Do
   you see a cup that's half full or a cup that's half-empty? Has
   your answer changed? And if it has, why do you think it has?

28

4. *Post-listening*: Match the numbers on the left with the letters on the right to find explanations for the new vocabulary. ANSWERS: 1-e 2-g 3-f 4-a 5-d 6-m 7-l 8-j 9-h 10-c 11-k 12-n 13-i 14-b

5. Fill in the gaps with words from the story. ANSWERS: 1 criticise 2 proud 3 apologise 4 gather 5 compassion 6 ashamed 7 remind 8 accomplish

COMMENTS
All of us feel like cracked pots at some time in our lives. Perhaps we suffer from depression, or have a physical challenge that limits our activity. Maybe we have suffered losses, or are unable to work full time as we think we should. But perhaps we need to honour the light that has come to us as a result of those things that we or others judge as flaws. Dr. Carl Jung suggested something to the effect that, it is not how we overcome our life challenges that is in the end important, but how we live with them and perhaps that is what this folk tale from India is all about.

The Cracked Pot

Once upon a time there was a man whose job was to bring water from the stream to his Master's house. The man carried the water from the stream in two clay pots. He hung the pots on each end of a pole, which he carried across his shoulders, to and from the stream many times a day.

One of the clay pots was perfect in every way for its purpose. The other pot was exactly like the first one, but it had a crack in it and it leaked. When the water bearer reached his Master's house, the perfect pot was always full, and the cracked pot was always half full.

The perfect pot was proud of its accomplishments, and it boasted loudly. It criticized the cracked pot for its failures, and reminded it that despite his efforts, the water bearer could only deliver half a pot of water due to his cracks. The poor cracked pot was ashamed of its imperfections, and was miserable that it could only accomplish half of what it was supposed to do.

One day the cracked pot spoke to the water bearer. "I want to apologize to you. Because of my cracked side I've only been able to deliver half of the water to your Master's home, and you don't get the full value from your efforts."

The water bearer smiled on the cracked pot, and in his compassion he said, "As we return to the Master's house, I want you to notice the beautiful flowers along the path."

Indeed as they climbed the path from the river to the Master's mansion the cracked pot took notice of the sun warming the beautiful flowers along one side of the path, and it felt somewhat brighter. But when they reached their destination and the water in the half-empty pot was poured out, his sadness returned. "Thank you for trying to cheer me up with the beautiful flowers, water bearer," The pot spoke. "But I still must apologize for my failure."

The water bearer said, "Dear pot, you haven't understood what I was trying to show you. Did you notice that the flowers only grew on your side of the path? That's because of your crack. I planted flower seeds on your side of the path, and everyday as we walked from the stream the water that leaks from your pot has watered them. I could have got a new pot, but I preferred to gather the flowers, and with them to bless many tables."

Worksheet: The Cracked Pot

Match the numbers on the left with the letters on the right to find explanations for the new vocabulary:

1.	clay	a.	allow liquid to escape when it should not
2.	pole	b.	collect
3.	a crack	c.	felt bad about
4.	leaked	d.	felt good about
5.	proud of	e.	heavy soil used for making pots
6.	accomplishments	f.	a line on the surface of something damaged
7.	boasted	g.	a long thin stick
8.	criticised	h.	made him think
9.	reminded	i.	make me feel better
10.	ashamed of	j.	said bad things about
11.	apologise	k.	say sorry
12.	mansion	l.	talked in a big-headed way
13.	cheer me up	m.	the things someone is able to do
14.	gather	n.	a very large house

Fill in the gaps with words from the story:

1. Why do you always _____ me for what I've done? I could do with some encouragement for a change!

2. I hear that your daughter has been awarded a scholarship. You must be very _____ of her.

3. Even if you _____ I can't forgive you because what you did was totally unacceptable.

4. I _____ your husband hasn't been feeling very well recently. I hope it's nothing serious.

5. Why do you have to be so hard-hearted? It wouldn't hurt you to show some _____ for a change.

6. How could he steal money from his own mother? He should be _____ of himself.

7. When you look at me like that you _____ me of my father.

8. I'm feeling a bit disappointed because I haven't been able to _____ as much as I had hoped.

Are we born into this world with a mission to make the most out of it for ourselves, or to leave something behind for others? And what would you like to be remembered for by others when you die? Perhaps the story that follows will help to provide the answers:

The Old Man and the Tree

An old man was planting a walnut tree.

A passer-by asked, "How old are you?"

"I'm eighty."

"And how long will it be before it's possible to eat the fruit from the tree that you're planting?"

"It will take forty years," the old man replied.

"So, and I hope you don't mind my pointing this out, do you really expect to live another forty years until you can enjoy these fruits?" asked the passer-by.

"No, of course I don't. But I've already been enjoying the fruits of the trees planted by my forefathers, and our children will enjoy the fruits of the tree that I plant", was the old man's answer.

***

This rewrite was based on a version of the story recorded by D. Atayev in the village of Khunzakh in 1952, found in *Avar Folk Tales* (Russian edition published by Nauka Publishing House, Moscow 1971, translated by D.G. Hunt). Ancient literary evidence of the same tale, in the Jewish-Aramaic language is noted by Gaster, M. (1924) in *The Exempla of the Rabbis*, London-Leipzig.

***

Another story from the Caucasus concludes the chapter, this time from Chechnya.

How Tamerlane Found His Fortune

One day Temir, whose horse was lame and had lost his son, called on a blacksmith. At that time the blacksmith was sleeping, and Temir, not wanting to disturb him, sat down by his side, waiting for him to wake up. He noticed that a fly came out of the blacksmith's nose, crawled along the tongs across a basin to the anvil. Beyond the anvil there was a huge fissure; the fly descended into this fissure and remained there quite a long time. Then it crawled back out and, after passing the anvil, crossed the basin by the same tongs, but while crossing it fell into the water. For a long time it was struggling in the water, but eventually it somehow managed to crawl out of the basin, and went back into the nose of the blacksmith again.

"It seems I've been asleep for quite some time!" "Yes, and I've been sitting waiting all that time". Temir replied. Amuse me. I've lost my son, my horse has pulled up lame and I've really had enough of everything today. Tell me something to take my mind off things and to cheer me up a bit". "But what can I tell you?" The blacksmith answered. After all, nobody can ever possibly obtain what I've just seen in my dream, and it would just make you even more frustrated". Temir asked him, nevertheless, to relate what he had experienced, and so the blacksmith did.

"In my dream I crossed a big river and an iron mountain and went down into a large cave, where there was treasure of gold and silver; for a long time I stood there, not having the strength to tear my eyes away from the brilliance and the splendour. But being conscious that I had to return, I climbed out of the cave. On the return journey when I was crossing the river, I fell off the bridge and almost drowned".

It was then Temir realised that it was the soul of the black-smith which had come out in the form of a fly. And guessing that there had to be some great treasure in the smithy, he persuaded the blacksmith to give the place up to him. Then after digging up the very same spot where the soul of the blacksmith had crawled, Temir exposed untold wealth, with which he collected an army and subjugated the whole world (adapted from Dalgat, 2004, pp.39-40).

***

What this traditional folktale shows is the ancient Ingush belief in the reality of dreams and how the soul for them was something material rather than an abstract concept. In fact, what it reflects, is an understanding of the soul that is remarkably similar to that of the Siberian Buryats. There is even a parallel Buryat tale in which the soul takes the form of a bee when it crawls out of someone's nose for an out-of-body experience (see Dalgat, 2004, p.40)

Notes for teachers

Pre-listening: Tell the person sitting next to you about a dream you've had that changed your life in some way, or about a remarkable dream that somebody you know had.

While-listening: Pause after the words "Then after digging up the very same spot where the soul of the blacksmith had crawled, Temir exposed ..." and ask the learners to predict the ending.

Post-listening: Now invite the learners, while working in groups, to write a parallel story about a fly that crawls out of someone's nose, the journey it goes on, and the discovery that journey eventually leads to for the dreamer.

***

The story is an adaptation of one found in the following book: Dalgat, B.K. (2004) *The Aboriginal Religions of the Chechens and Ingush*, Moscow: NAUKA. (Translated from the Russian by David Hunt, October 2009, and now in the British Library. The book was first published in an abridged form in 1893).

4

Lead-ins to New Topics

Pairwork interviews can be used as a lead-in to a new topic, and some sets are presented below as examples. You will notice that instead of the teacher deciding on the questions to be discussed, with this type of activity the students are given more of a choice in the matter. When working with larger classes, the learners can then be arranged in circles of eight for the reporting stage, and you can move among the groups.

What I do while listening to the reports is to make notes in two columns, on a sheet of paper or an OHT, of the effective language used and also of the problems that reveal themselves. At the end of the lesson, so as not to interrupt the flow during the productive stage, I then go through these together with the class as a whole. First of all, I focus on the effective language that was produced to provide the learners with positive "strokes", and then point out the errors, asking them to self-correct if possible and to explain why the utterances were problematic. Obviously this has to be done selectively, just focussing on those points you consider to be the most important to deal with, taking the students' needs and level into account, so as not to undermine their self-confidence in their ability to get their message across. The last thing you want to do is to inhibit the learners from practising their English, which is why it is important not to overdo the error correction. The aim is to promote fluency, but not at the expense of accuracy.

Obviously, if you used the same kind of activity as a lead-in to every topic you introduce, the learners would soon get bored with the approach, and there are many other options available to you. You could use a song, a story, a set of cartoons, a reading text, an audio or video recording, an information gap activity, a questionnaire – the list of possibilities is endless. Remember that variety is the spice of life, and that if the learning experience you create is a memorable one, it is that much more likely to be retained and then available for recall by those you work with.

Please note that the sets of questions presented below were originally developed for learners studying in the UK, and for use in other settings they may need to be adapted.

Pick out three questions that interest you to ask the person you are sitting next to, and then report back with what you find out to the rest of the class:

a. What has your experience of the NHS (the National Health Service) been like? Are you impressed with the service you have received Is medical carehere from doctors? Tell me about it.

b. If you were seriously ill, would you make use of the NHS or would you pay to have private treatment? Give your reasons.

c. Is medical care free in your country? What system is there in place, and what do you think of it?

d. What changes would you introduce if you were Minister of Health? Give your reasons.

e. If you had a terminal illness, would you want your doctor to tell you the truth? Why or why not?

f. How do you feel about alternative medicine – the use of homoeopathy or acupuncture, for example? What experience do you have of such treatment? Tell me about it.

g. What do you do on a personal level to keep fit and deal with stress?

h. How do you feel about cosmetic surgery, and would you ever consider having it? Why or why not?

i. Life expectancy is increasing all the time and people are now living into their eighties on average in Europe. What are the consequences of this likely to be?

j. Should retirement be compulsory once people reach a certain age and, if you think so, when?

k. When you die, what would you like to be remembered for?

l. It has been suggested that people who persist in smoking should be refused NHS treatment. What do you think?

m. How do you feel about vegetarianism? Are you one or would you consider becoming one? Why or why not?

Pick out three questions that interest you to ask the person you are sitting next to, and then report back with what you find out to the rest of the class:

a. Are you optimistic or pessimistic about the future of our planet? Give your reasons.

b. It has been suggested that we are here to be caretakers of this planet and it is our duty to look after it for our children and our children's children. What do you think?

c. Do you believe in life after death? If so, what form do you think it takes?

d. How do you feel about methods to predict the future – astrology, palmistry, clairvoyance, tarot cards etc? Have you ever been to a fortune teller for a consultation? And, if so, were the predictions made accurate?

e. Have you ever had a premonition that came true? If so, tell me about it.

f. How often do you read your horoscope? Are you typical of your sign and do you know which sign you are compatible with?

g. "Space exploration is a complete waste of money as it would be much better spent on developing alternative forms of energy." What do you think?

h. Is there life on other planets – what do you think? And if there is, do you think it is more or less intelligent than we are?

i. Is our future pre-determined or can we control the direction it takes? What do you think?

j. Ghosts and witches – are there any legends from your country about them, have you ever encountered one or do you know anybody who has? If so, tell me about it.

k. Have you ever taken part in a séance or do you know anybody who has? Tell me about it. And if you have never taken part in a séance, would you consider doing so if you were invited to?

Pick out three questions that interest you to ask the person you are sitting next to, and then report back with what you find out to the rest of the class:

a. When you go shopping, which items do you tend to spend most money on?

b. Where do you usually buy your clothes – locally, in exclusive designer label shops, in department stores, in sales, in street markets or in charity shops?

c. When you go shopping, do you tend to pay cash, use a credit card or use a debit card? And why do you prefer this method?

d. Do you buy in shops where you know the people who make the clothes they sell are probably paid less than the minimum wage for what they do?

e. When you go shopping for food, do you look for Fair Trade coffee and tea, buy the cheapest you can find, or only buy one particular brand because it's your favourite?

f. Have you ever worked as an assistant in a shop? And if you haven't, would you like to? Why or why not?

g. Do you buy organic fruit and vegetables because they are better for the environment and your health or do you simply buy the cheapest you can find? Give reasons for the choice you make.

h. How do you feel about shoplifting and shoplifters? Do you think it makes a difference if the guilty person is poor rather than wealthy? Have you ever taken anything without paying? Tell me about it.

i. If you were given too much change in a shop by mistake, would you keep it or return it to the assistant?

j. If your partner bought some new clothes that looked awful and they asked you what you thought of them, would you tell them the truth or a white lie so as not to hurt their feelings? And if you were in the same position, what would you prefer to be told?

k. How do you feel about having to haggle over prices? Are you prepared to do it or would you prefer to shop elsewhere instead, where the prices are fixed?

l. Would you describe yourself as being an extravagant shopper and a big spender, or do you only buy what you really need?

Pick out three questions that interest you to ask the person you are sitting next to, and then report back with what you find out to the rest of the class:

a. They say that the English love animals more than children. In your experience, how accurate would you say this observation is?

b. How do you feel about blood sports such as bullfighting or fox hunting?

c. When it's time to eat in your household, who do you feed first, and why – your family, your pets or yourself?

d. "I never buy any products that have been tested on animals." Is this a statement you could make?

e. Would you be prepared to become a vegetarian or a vegan? Why or why not?

f. Some vegetarians oblige their pet dogs and cats to eat only vegetarian food too. How do you feel about this?

g. Free range eggs or eggs produced as a result of battery farming – what do you buy, and why?

h. How do you feel about animals being slaughtered to make fur coats from their skins and would you be prepared to buy one?

i. Some people say that zoos are nothing more than prisons for animals and serve no useful purpose, which is why they should all be closed. What do you think?

j. Which charity would you rather donate money to – an organisation that supports the rights of tribal peoples, a charity that supports cancer research, an organisation that works to prevent cruelty to animals, or perhaps a different charity you feel strongly about?

k. Forcing animals to perform tricks in circuses or on stage is both cruel and degrading, which is why legislation should be introduced to prohibit such shows. What do you think?

l. If you could be born again as an animal, which animal would you like to be, and why?

Pick out three questions that interest you to ask the person you are sitting next to, and then report back with what you find out to the rest of the class:

a. "Travel broadens the mind" or "There's no place like home" – which of these sayings best represents the way you feel about travel?

b. If you had an unlimited amount of money to spend on a holiday, where would you choose to go, and why?

c. A package holiday with an all inclusive hotel stay or independent travel? What would you be more inclined to go for? Give your reasons.

d. Tell me about the most unforgettable holiday you have ever had. What was so special about it?

e. What can you do, or do you do, to reduce your carbon footprint when travelling?

f. A luxurious five star hotel or a camping site – what would your preference be for? Give your reasons.

g. Some people say that the only way to learn about another country and the culture of its people is by living and working there. What do you think?

h. Are you the sort of person who plans trips in meticulous detail months in advance or do you book your holidays at the very last minute?

i. "It's better to travel hopefully than to arrive." – What do you think?

j. Lazing around on the beach all day or visiting places of interest – how do you prefer to spend your holiday? Give your reasons.

k. What were your first impressions when you arrived in this country for the first time? And have they changed since then?

l. When it comes to food on holiday, do you stick to tried and tested favourites (fish and chips if you're British, for example) or do you prefer to experiment and to try something different? And what's the strangest food you've ever tried on your travels?

m. Do you have any regrets about coming to this country? And if you could have your time over again, what would you choose to do differently?

Pick out three questions that interest you to ask the person you are sitting next to, and then report back with what you find out to the rest of the class:

a. What qualities do you look for in a partner, and what qualities do you feel you have to offer?

b. Some people say you can only expect to find true love once in your life. What do you think?

c. How do you feel about lonely hearts ads and speed dating? Would you be prepared to look for a partner this way or do you know anyone who has?

d. They say that absence makes the heart grow fonder. What has your experience been?

e. How important do you think faithfulness in a relationship to be, and what would you do if you found out your partner was cheating on you?

f. Why do you think so many marriages seem to end up in divorce these days?

g. Do you believe in love at first sight? What has your experience been?

h. Should gay couples be allowed to get married to each other and to adopt children – what do you think?

i. They say blood is thicker than water. What do you think? And how important are you friends to you – more important than your family or less important?

j. They say that long distance relationships, when both partners are required to live in different countries, rarely work. What do you think? Do you know anyone in this situation or have you ever been in a situation like this?

k. When you move to a foreign country, what do you think is the best way of making new friends? What advice would you give to someone coming to England for the first time?

l. A lot of couples prefer living together these days instead of getting married. How do you feel about this?

Pick out three questions that interest you to ask the person you are sitting next to, and then report back with what you find out to the rest of the class:

a. They say that money can't buy you love, health or happiness. What do you think?

b. What does the government do in your country to support people who are out of work?

c. Do you ever give money to beggars or buskers? Why or why not?

d. Would you describe yourself as a generous person when it comes to spending money or do you tend to be rather tight-fisted?

e. If you won the lottery, would you be likely to carry on working or would you retire? And if you retired, what would you then like to do with your time?

f. What would you describe as your greatest extravagance?

g. If a fire broke out in your house and you had to leave it in a hurry, what would you try to save first, and why?

h. When looking for work, what is your main concern – the salary, the hours, the holidays, or whether it would provide you with job satisfaction or not?

i. How do you feel about paying for goods or services over the Internet? Would you, for example, choose and pay for a holiday this way?

j. Given the current economic climate, what would you advise people to do with any money they manage to save?

k. What charities do you support on a regular basis and, if you don't support any, then why not?

l. How often do money problems keep you awake at night? And if it's a regular problem with sleeping that you have, what are you doing to solve it?

Pick out three questions that interest you to ask the person you are sitting next to, and then report back with what you find out to the rest of the class:

a. It has been said that prisons are nothing more than Universities of Crime. What do you think?

b. Have you ever been in prison or do you know anybody who has? Tell me about it.

c. They say that crime doesn't pay. How far do you agree with this statement?

d. Do you believe the police should be allowed to carry guns at all times or only in certain circumstances?

e. Some people say that in effect there are two legal systems in operation – one for the rich and another for the poor. What is your opinion on the subject?

f. Have you ever been found guilty of breaking the law? Tell me about it.

g. Some people say that life imprisonment should mean life. What do you think?

h. In some countries capital punishment still takes place. How do you feel about it?

i. Paedophiles have been in the news a lot recently. Some people believe they should be castrated. What do you think?

j. One form of justice is an eye for an eye and a tooth for a tooth. How do you feel about this approach to dealing with crime?

k. What do you think should be done about illegal workers in this country? It has been suggested that there should be an amnesty for them so that they can work officially and the country can benefit from the taxes they will then be required to pay. What do you think of this idea?

l. As an employer, would you be prepared to give someone a job if you knew they had a criminal record?

Pick out three questions that interest you to ask the person you are sitting next to, and then report back with what you find out to the rest of the class:

a. Tell me about a book, film, or play that has significantly changed your life in some way.

b. If you had the choice, which famous writer from the present (or the past) would you like to meet, and what would you like to ask him or her?

c. Which newspapers, if any, do you read on a regular basis, and which ones do you avoid?

d. What do you prefer – going to the cinema or going to the theatre? And tell me about the last film or play you went to see.

e. How much attention do you pay to the gossip pages in your daily newspaper?

f. Are there any magazines you read on a regular basis or

journals you subscribe to? Tell me about them.

g. Do you think there should be some form of censorship of the arts or should everything be allowed?

h. How do you feel about the showing of adverts for cigarettes, alcohol, and junk food on television and in the cinema?

i. Should all galleries and museums be free or should we have to pay an entrance fee to enjoy our great works of art?

j. Should the government subsidise opera and ballet companies or should they be required to sink or swim on their own?

k. What page do you turn to first in your daily paper, and which page or pages do you never read?

l. Tell me about a song or a piece of music that holds special memories for you.

Pick out three questions that interest you to ask the person you are sitting next to, and then report back with what you find out to the rest of the class:

a. What do you consider to be more valuable, and why – the education we get from books or the education we get from life?

b. Tell me about a teacher you have had or a book you have read that has significantly changed your life in some way.

c. Should university education be free for everyone or should both undergraduate and post-graduate students be required to pay fees?

d. It has been suggested that prisons are universities – Universities of Crime. How far do you agree with this?

e. Have you ever cheated in an exam or do you know anyone who has, and can cheating in such circumstance ever be justified?

f. Should students from non EU countries be required to pay higher university fees than EU students, or should the fees be the same for everyone?

g. As the cost of university education is so high, and as there is no guarantee that it will lead to employment, is there really any point in going to University any more?

h. Do you prefer studying in a class with a group of students or having one-to-one classes? And what do you think is the reason for this?

i. What do you look for when choosing a language school, and what do you look for in a teacher?

j. Is it possible for a teacher to change pupils or students by pressurising them into making changes or do you believe we can only learn form our own mistakes?

k. As nobody can produce their best work under exam conditions, all traditional exams should be replaced with a system of continuous assessment. What do you think?

l. In a classroom situation, do you prefer working on your

own, in pairs or in groups?

m. Based on your own experience, what advice would you give to someone who was planning to (come to the UK to) study English for the first time?

Pick out three questions that interest you to ask the person you are sitting next to, and then report back with what you find out to the rest of the class:

a. They say that a healthy body is a healthy mind. How far do you agree with this, and what do you do on a regular basis to keep yourself fit?

b. Should sports be a compulsory subject in schools – what do you think?

c. A lot of people think professional footballers are grossly overpaid and that there should be a limit imposed on how much they earn. What do you think?

d. Motor racing should be banned as it is not only wasteful of natural resources and of money that can be better spent, but also encourages a love of speed that leads to dangerous driving. What do you think of this suggestion?

e. Have you, or has anyone close to you, ever won any medals or cups for achievements in athletics or on the sports field? Tell me about it.

f. What sportspeople and celebrities get up to in private is their own business and we have no right to pass judgement on them based on what they do in the other areas of their lives. What do you think?

g. How patriotic are you when it comes to supporting your national sports teams or athletes, and how do you feel about National Anthems being played before important football matches or at the awards ceremonies in the Olympics?

h. What do you think should be done about sports people if they are caught taking drugs to enhance their performances? What changes to the current legislation would you like to see take place?

i. Blood sports such as bull fighting and fox hunting are barbarous and should be unequivocally banned. How far do you agree with this?

j. How competitive are you? Do you take the attitude that winning is everything or is the fun of just taking part more important to you?

k. Is there any limit to how fast man can run or will world records in athletics always continue to fall? What do you think?

l. What do you do to help you relax, and is there a particular technique you use that you could teach me – a breathing exercise for example?

How honest are you?

Discuss the following questions in small groups, and then elect a spokesperson to present your findings to the rest of the class:

a. Is lying ever justifiable and, if so, when?

b. When was the last time you told a lie? Tell me about it.

c. Are certain kinds of lies more acceptable than others or are all lies morally wrong?

d. If you were found to be terminally ill, would you want your doctor to tell you the truth or to tell you that you were going to get better so as to give you some hope?

e. Would you prefer a partner who was always straight with you and told you the truth or one who would tell you white lies from time to time so as not to hurt your feelings?

f. If you interviewed someone for a job and they turned out to be unsuitable, would you tell them why face to face, tell them in a letter, or tell them they had been unsuccessful but without giving them a reason for your decision?

g. Would you prefer your teacher to tell you if your work was sub-standard and if you were likely to fail your exams, or to encourage you by saying there is always hope so keep on trying?

h. Imagine you worked in a fashionable clothes shop and a customer tried on a really expensive dress that looked absolutely hideous on them. Would you tell them it looked great in order to sell it and make a fat commission or would you advise them against buying it?

i. If you had a partner and a family to support and found yourself out of work and in severe financial difficulty, would you lie at an interview in order to get a job or would you still tell the interviewer the truth even if it resulted in your not getting selected?

j. How do you feel about cheating in exams and have you ever done so? Tell me about it.

The weather and the environment

Discuss the following questions in small groups, and then elect a spokesperson to present your findings to the rest of the class:

a. They say that English people always talk about the weather – true or false?

b. What is your favourite season of the year, and why?

c. They say that climate affects the kind of people we are. People from hot countries, for example, tend to be more passionate – true or false?

d. Do you bother to listen, or read, the weather forecast each day? Why or why not?

e. What does S.A.D. stand for, and do you suffer from it?

f. How concerned are you about the damage currently being done to the environment?

g. What are you doing on a personal level about it, and what would you like to see the government do?

h. Do you think we have a future to look forward to, or is the world coming to an end?

i. Have you ever voted for the Green Party? Why or why not?

j. If you knew the world was going to end tomorrow, how would you spend today?

k. What is a "carbon footprint" and what are you doing to keep yours under control?

Short newspaper articles can be used for lead-ins to work on new topics too, especially those that deal with controversial issues like the two examples presented below:

Call for a 21-hour working week

It has been suggested that the working week should be cut to 21 hours to help boost the economy and improve quality of life as the reduction in hours would help to ease both unemployment and overwork. After all, it makes no sense that people are working longer hours now than 30 years ago when unemployment was so high.

True people would earn less, but they would have more time to carry out worthy tasks ahead. They would have better scope to look after children or other dependents, there would be, there would be more opportunity for civic duties, and older people could even delay retirement if this reduction in the number of working hours was introduced.

So many of us live to work, work to earn, and earn to consumes, and our consumption habits are squandering the earth's natural resources. Spending less time in paid work could help us to break this pattern. This way we would have more time to be better parents, better citizens, better carers and better neighbours. We could even become better employees – less strained, more in control, happier in our jobs and more productive. It is time to break the power of the old industrial clock, take back our lives and work for a sustainable future.

Although a cultural shift of this magnitude will throw up real challenges, there could also be enormous benefits – for our economy, for our quality of life and, above all, for our planet.

What do you think? Discuss this suggestion in small groups and then elect a spokesperson to present your conclusions to the rest of the class. Alternatively, write a proposal with your recommendations – either for a change in the law or for leaving things the way they currently are.

Concern grows over gambling in the UK

There is growing concern over the number of people turning to gambling to survive the recession. Research shows that nearly 1 in 10 adults in the UK has used gambling as a way to manage their finances and make extra money.

People have to pay their mortgage and electricity bills, but they do not know where to get the finance to do that if they have not got enough at the end of the month, so what happens is that they turn to gambling in desperation.

The trend of more people using gambling to get through tough times for their finances is being seen by gambling support groups too, and gambling counselling services see first-hand evidence of it. People go to them with the irrational thought pattern that gambling is a good way of getting money. In reality, though, it is just a good way of increasing your debt. And once people start in that cycle of gambling, the ironic thing is it is often seen by them as the only way out of the problem.

Gambling addicts say it gives them an excitement, a buzz, and that sort of stuff, so they carry on playing. They just completely lose their minds thinking that they are going to win and that they are unbeatable, and the problem is on the rise.

Many of the people looking for help with gambling addictions are students. The number of people looking for help with betting problems is up by more than 20% in a year, according to a charity dealing with gambling addicts. To make matters even more worrying, more than a thir of those who get in touch are apparently aged between 18 and 25 and many are students.

They gamble away their grants and then they start borrowing or even stealing from friends. They steal from their families too. They get into so much difficulty that in the end they lose so much that some are even forced to give up their studies. Moreover, students are getting increasingly hooked to online gambling to try to pay off their loans.

One of the problems is that there are so many enticements to gamble. You can gamble on almost anything you want from the internet, through to fruit machines, through to horse race betting. And the government does hardly anything to discourage it as it provides a major source of income, in the same way as the tax on cigarettes and alcohol does.

***

Should the government introduce new legislation to make all forms of gambling for money illegal – what do you think? Discuss what should be done, if anything, about the problem in small groups and then elect a spokesperson to present your views to the rest of the class. Alternatively, write a short story entitled "How I lost a Fortune but found my Calling in Life"

Finally, a short story that could be used as a possible lead-in to the topic of education:

What do you consider to be more valuable, and why – the education we get from books or the education we get from life? Perhaps the answer lies in this traditional Georgian tale. It is an adaptation of a story that was originally translated by

Marjory Wardrop, sister of the 19th century british diplomat and scholar of Georgia, Sir Oliver Wardrop.

The man of books (who died) and the captain of the ship (who survived)

Once upon a time, an educated man, an academic, was on board a ship when there was a great storm. While the storm was raging he heard the captain giving various orders to the members of the crew, but he could not understand a word. So when the danger was past, he asked the captain what language he had spoken in, to which he replied: "In my mother tongue, of course!" The scholar then expressed his regret that a man should have wasted half his life without learning how to speak properly – grammatically and intelligibly. A few hours later the storm arose again, and this time the ship sprang a leak and began to sink. This time it was the captain who approached the scholar and asked him if he could swim. The man of books replied that unfortunately he had never learned how to. "In that case, I am truly sorry, sir, and you had better say your prayers for you are about to lose your life. The ship will go down to the bottom in a minute, and my crew and I shall swim ashore. So it seems it would have been a lot better for you if you had spent a little of your time, instead of reading books, in learning how to swim."

Reference

Wardrop, Marjory (Tr.) (1894) *Georgian Folk Tales*, London: David Nutt in the Stand.

5

How to Write a Formal Letter
(A Lesson Plan)

Objectives

To provide the preparatory work necessary to facilitate the writing of formal letters. An ordering activity will be used to present the recommended lay-out of such letters. A "Spot the Mistakes" exercise will be used to focus on common errors and a relatively easy Questionnaire will be set in which success should be assured to help promote positive self-esteem.

Activities

The lesson consists of three stages that are outlined below:

1. An ordering activity for group work with cards: Each group will be given a set of cards to order and I will circulate during the activity to provide any assistance required. This caters for the Bodily-kinaesthetic Intelligence Type – for those of us who learn through movement. The correct version will then be displayed on the OHP. **Timing 15 minutes**

2. Find the deliberate mistakes for pair work: To vary the forms of interaction, this time the learners will be asked to work on the activity in pairs and photocopies will be provided. The correct answers will then be elicited, making use of the OHP once again. **Timing 20 minutes**

3. A Questionnaire through which the learner can find out how much they know about letter writing: The students can work on this individually and photocopies will be provided for this purpose. The incentive of a fabulous mystery prize will be offered as a carrot for the winner! **Timing: 15 minutes**

Materials

27 Cavendish Road
London NW6 2DT

The Personnel Officer
Secure Guards Ltd
320 The High Street
London SE8 0ER

20/6/2011

Dear sir,

I am applying for the post of Security Guard advertised in "The Daily Standard" yesterday and I am enclosing a copy of my CV as requested.

As you can see, I have worked for five years as the Prime Minister's personal bodyguard and before that I was in the army. My commanding officer and the Prime Minister can both supply you with references and their addresses can be found on my CV.

My experience in the army included working in Iraq and Afghanistan. I have also accompanied the Prime Minister on his overseas trips. I notice that the advertised vacancy involves working overseas and I am very keen on travelling, which is why I have chosen to apply for this post.

I hope you will give my application serious consideration and I look forward to hearing from you.

Yours faithfully,

Richard Strong

Richard Strong

How not to write a formal letter!

There are grammar mistakes, spelling mistakes, punctuation mistakes, mistakes in the order of the paragraphs, and also mistakes in the lay-out. Work in pairs and see how many you can find!

19 avenue road
Ealing W6 OER

Majestic Hotel
Bournemouth
Hampshire HR4 PMT

The nineteenth of January

dear Julia Rambert,

I am interesting in the job of Waitress advertised on "Metro" this morning and I am enclosing a copy of my CV.
I hope you will consider my application carefuly and I look forward to hear from you.

I am working as waitress in my own country since five years before I came here and my former employer can provide you with a referee.

I imagine that you cater mainly for overseas tourists so I belief my language skills would be usefull. In addition to speak both portuguese and english, I also can understand spanish.

yours faithfully,

Maria Chagas

Maria Chagas

19 Avenue Road
Ealing W6 OER

The Majestic Hotel
Bournemouth
Hampshire HR4 PMT

19/6/2011

Dear Julia Rambert,

I am interested in the job of Waitress advertised in "Metro" this morning and I am enclosing a copy of my CV.

I worked as a waitress in my own country for five years before I came here and my former employer can provide you with a reference.
I imagine that you cater mainly for overseas tourists so I believe my language skills would be useful. In addition to speaking both Portuguese and English, I can also understand Spanish.

I hope you will consider my application carefully and I look forward to hearing from you.

Yours sincerely,

Maria Chagas

Maria Chagas

How much do you know about writing Formal Letters?

Read the following statements, and then decide if they are true or false:

1.   When the letter starts *Dear sir* we end it with *Yours sincerely,*

2. You can end a letter to someone you know with *Best wishes,*

3. The first paragraph of the letter should explain your reason for writing.

4. You should start a new paragraph for each sentence.

5. You should leave a space between each paragraph.

6. *Ms* is the title used for a married woman.

7. *Master* is the title used for a man.

8. If you are writing a formal letter, it is not a good idea to use contractions. (*I'm* is the contraction of *I am*; *can't* is the contraction of *cannot*)

9. When you are writing an application for a job, it is a good idea to say what a wonderful person you are. For example, *I am intelligent, honest and I work very hard.*

10. When you apply for a job, it is a good idea to use a recycled envelope.

6

The Prince Who Thought
He Was a Turkey: NLP Revisited

NLP stands for Neuro-Linguistic Programming. It has been described as the practical psychology of how to use the mind to consistently achieve goals in all areas of life. Neuro refers to the nervous system by which our experiences are processed via the five senses. Linguistic refers to language and also non-verbal communication systems through which our experiences are coded, ordered and given meaning. Programming refers to the ability to discover, utilise and change the patterns that we run in our thinking, feeling and behaving. Your thinking and feeling shape your experience of the world. Changing the patterns of your thinking and feeling changes your reality, and the aim of NLP is to change it for the better.

NLP was first developed at the University of California, Santa Cruz in the period of 1973-1979, where John Grinder, Richard Bandler, and Gregory Bateson were all based.

Rapport is the foundation for any meaningful interaction between two or more people – rapport is about establishing an environment of trust and understanding, to respect and honour the other person's world, which gives a person the freedom to fully express their ideas and concerns and to know they will be respected by the other person(s).

Most of our communication, as much as 93%, transpires non-verbally and unconsciously. NLP rapport skills teach us how to communicate at that unconscious level. The key to establishing rapport is an ability to enter another person's world by assuming a similar state of mind. The first thing to do is to become more like the other person by matching and mirroring the person's behaviours. Matching and mirroring is a powerful way of getting an appreciation of how the other person is seeing/experiencing the world. If your partner is using many visual words, you should also use mainly visual words and similarly for auditory, kinaesthetic and auditory digital words.

There is, however, nothing new about this knowledge, as the following story, written more than two hundred years ago, clearly illustrates. This story, by Rabbi Nachman of Bratislav, the great grandson of the Baal Shem Tov, was adapted from Shulman, Y.D. (1993) *The Chambers of the Palace: Teachings of Rabbi Nachman of Bratislav*, Northvale, New Jersey: Jason Aronson Inc.

The Prince Who Thought He Was a Turkey

Once there was a prince who thought he was a turkey. He sat naked underneath a table and pecked at bones and pieces of bread. All the doctors despaired of healing him, and the king was very sad.

Then a wise man came and said, "Don't worry. I've got the answer to the problem. Just watch and do what I tell you."

The wise man took off his clothes and sat under the table next to the prince, and he also pecked at crumbs and bones.

The prince asked him, "Who are you? What are you doing here?"

The wise man answered, "And what are you doing here?"

"I'm a rooster."

"I'm also a rooster."

The two of them sat there for some time until they got used to each other. Then the wise man gave a signal, and a shirt was thrown down.

The wise man said to the prince, "Do you think that a rooster can't wear a shirt? One can wear a shirt and still be a rooster."

So both of them put on shirts.

After a while, he signalled again, and a pair of trousers was thrown down to him.

He said, "Do you think if someone wears pants, he can't be a rooster?"

This went on until they were both dressed.

Afterwards, he signalled, and human food was thrown down from the table. He said to the prince, "Do you think if you eat good food, you're no longer a turkey? One can eat and still be a turkey." So they both ate.

After that, he told the prince. "Do you think that a turkey can only sit under the table? One can sit at the table and still be a turkey."

And he continued to act in this way until he completely cured the prince.

***

If you plan to use the story in class, then here is a possible follow-up activity that could actually be used with any story you ever tell a group of students.

Choose a couple of the following questions to ask the person sitting next to you. Then report back what you found out to the rest of the class:

a. What feelings did you have during the telling of the story?

b. Have you ever been in a similar situation to any of the characters in the tale?

c. Did any of the characters remind you of people you know?

d. What do you think the "message" of the story is?

e. Did it remind you of any other stories you know?

f. Which was the most moving or memorable bit of the story for you?

g. Which bit of the story sent you off to sleep?

***

Here are some further ideas for follow-up work that could be used for a teacher development workshop:

- If you were reborn as an animal, which animal would you like, or, wouldn't you like, to be and why?

- Have you ever known, or been taught by, a teacher you thought shouldn't have been one or who acted as if he/she was something else?

- Working in small groups, choose one of the following titles and write the story to accompany it:

The Teacher Who Thought He/She Knew All the Answers
The Teacher Who Thought He/She Was Unworthy
The Teacher Who Longed To Be Someone Else

(Ideally, the story should involve an intervention that brings about a change for the better to the poor miserable soul's condition).

***

Sometimes we can be our own worst enemies, placing unnecessary burdens on ourselves as a result of the language we use. However, by making use of reformulation, another NLP technique, we can change both our attitudes and our behaviour, as the following tale can be used to illustrate. First, however, before presenting the tale, a couple of questions for you to consider:

- Can you accept people the way they are or are you always trying to change them?

- Is it possible to change the way people think by pressurizing them or do you believe we can only learn from our own mistakes?

And now for the story itself:

The Man Who Always Said Should

He was always telling people what they should or shouldn't do and he knew best about everything. He didn't realize that *should* is probably the most damaging word in the English vocabulary. It implies you were wrong, you are wrong, or you're going to be wrong. What people really need is more choice in their lives, the choice offered by removing and replacing all *shoulds*.

At least you could say, he practised what he preached because he behaved the same way towards himself as he behaved towards everyone else. All the time the voice inside his own head was making statements about what he *should* and *shouldn't* do, how he *should* live his life and I suppose that's why he then imposed the same on others. Poor man. I wonder if he ever got any peace. Probably only when he was sleeping. And perhaps not even then. Who knows what he went through in his dreams? Probably constant torment. Not surprising then that he lost all his hair and ended up having a heart attack. But he didn't even learn from that. For once he'd recovered from the triple by-pass operation his condition necessitated, he started acting just as he had done before.

In fact, if anything, he became even more unbearable. To put up with him you had to be a saint. And that's exactly what his dear wife was.

However, gradually through his constant criticism, he destroyed even her. He hammered away at her daily until she no longer had any mind of her own. Her actions became dictated by what she thought he believed she *should* or *shouldn't* do. That's when he lost interest in her and left her for another woman – someone else to mould into his likeness. Three days later she killed herself.

After that he became a changed man. He got himself committed to an asylum, which suited him just fine. He was drugged up to the eyeballs daily, his nagging inner voice was silenced forever, and he no longer had to make any choices at all. They were all made for him there.

I suppose he's found peace of mind of a kind. He spends his days sitting glued to the TV watching soap operas. The only choice to be made is which channel to watch. And he doesn't even have to make that decision as the nurse on duty does that for him. No more *shoulds* or *shouldn'ts* to worry about and that's the way he likes it - much safer by far.

***

Make a list of all the things you think you should do. Give yourself a ten-minute time limit. Then reformulate the items in your lists by using the following wording:

If I really wanted to, I could ….

You will probably find some things now seem much more possible and there are others which you now want to abandon. *Could* gives you choice!

Now discuss your findings, working in pairs or small groups.

***

Every day God gives us the sun – and also one moment in which we have the ability to change everything that makes us unhappy. Every day, we try to pretend that we haven't perceived that moment, that it doesn't exist – that today is the same as yesterday and will be the same as tomorrow. But if people really pay attention to their everyday lives, they will discover that magic moment. (Taken from "By the River Piedra I Sat Down And Wept" by Paulo Coelho).

***

How do we respond when our set patterns are challenged through NLP or through any other form of therapy for that matter? Stepping out of the comfort zones we create for ourselves, however poorly they may in fact serve us, requires courage, and is a challenge we all have to come up against at some point in life.

One way to find the answer is by going within, which brings us on to the subject of guided visualisation, another technique employed by NLP practitioners which has been around for a very long time. In fact, it can be traced back to pre-Christian times, as it is very much what traditional shamans can be said to have practised, though in a less controlled form.

A shaman is understood to be someone who performs an ecstatic (in a trance state), imitative, or demonstrative ritual of a séance (or a combination of all three), at will (in other words, whenever he or she chooses to do so), in which aid is sought from beings in (what are considered to be) other realities generally for healing purposes or for divination – both for individuals and / or the community.

As for the practice of shamanism, it is understood to encompass a personalistic view of the world, in which life is seen to be not only about beliefs and practices, but also about relationships–how we are related, and how we relate to each other. In shamanism the notion of interdependence "is the idea of the kinship of all life, the recognition that nothing can exist in and of itself without being in relationship to other things, and therefore that it is insane for us to consider ourselves as essentially unrelated parts of the whole Earth" (Halifax in Nicholson, (comp.), 1987, p.220). And through neurotheology, this assertion so often heard expressed in neo-shamanic circles that all life is connected, can now be substantiated. This is because

> [I]t has been shown that during mystical ecstasy (or its equivalent, entheogenic shamanic states [states induced by ingesting hallucinogens]), the individual experiences a blurring of the boundaries on the ego and feels at "one with Nature"; the ego is no longer confined within the body, but extends outward to all of Nature; other living beings come to share in the ego, as an authentic communion with the environment, which is sensed as in some way divine (Ruck, Staples, et al., 2007, p.76).

Further justification for the belief that all life is connected can be found in the fact that the elementary particles that make up all matter, by their gravitational, electromagnetic or nuclear field, are coextensive with the whole universe, and as man is composed of these particles, he is thus in union with the entire cosmos (see Eliade, pp.285-286).

There is believed to be an built-in spiritual centre located among neural connections in the temporal lobes of the brain. Evidence to support this hypothesis is based on scans taken with positron emission topography, which show that these neural areas light up whenever subjects are exposed to discussion of religious or spiritual topics. Neurobiologists have now dubbed the area of the temporal lobes cond with religious or spiritual experience the 'God spot' or the 'God module'.

People who report religious experiences are more likely than others to display enhanced temporal lobe signs, and temporal lobe epilepsy is associated with particular types of religiosity, suggesting that this region of the brain affects religious functioning. Kenneth Dewhurst and A.W. Beard surveyed patients with temporal lobe epilepsy; 38% showed particular interest in religion after the onset of their illness compared to 8% who showed religious interest before the onset of illness (McClenon, 2002, p.90).

Other researchers in "neurotheology" (using brain imaging techniques to study spiritual contemplatives) have also observed that prayer and meditation can bring about a shift in brain activity associated with such unitive experiences as "the presence of God" and "oneness with the universe" (see Newberg, D'Aquili, & Rause, 2001, pp.115-116).

Peggy Ann Wright, 1995, working at Lesley College in Cambridge, Massachusetts, studied the link between heightened temporal lob activity and shamanistic experiences, and found that rhythmic drumming of the sort used in a vast range of spiritual rituals excites the temporal lobes and associated areas of the limbic system. However, rhythmic drumming is only one of many ways of accessing states for trance work. Guided visualisation can also be used to excite the temporal lobes and here is an example of a script that can be used in the classroom.

Taking Your Rightful Place at the Round Table

SCRIPT FOR THE GUIDE: (To be read in a gentle trance-inducing voice.) Make yourself comfortable and close your eyes. Take a few deep breaths to help you relax. Breathe in the light and breathe out all your tightness. Feel the tension disappear stage by stage from the top of your head to the tips of your toes. Let your surroundings fade away as you gradually sink backwards through time and actuality and pass through the gateway of reality into the dreamtime. (When the participants are fully relaxed, begin the next stage.)

Sometimes, like all of us, you probably consider yourself unworthy and can't resist the temptation to compare yourself to others. Not to worry because help is close at hand, probably closer than you realize.

You enter the doorway of what appears to be some kind of temple or parliament building. Your name is being called and you hear a fanfare of trumpets. You walk down the central aisle. Smell the incense being burned. Each of the stained glass windows in the walls depicts a scene from history – pictures of all the great artists, writers, composers, scientists, politicians, inventors and discoverers. Take a minute of clock time, equal to all the time you need, to study the pictures ....

At the far end you see an enormous round table. All the seats are taken except for one. You look around at the faces and see all the people you've ever admired seated in a circle. Who should be sitting in the empty chair? Wait a minute. The people at the table seem to be pointing in your direction. You look behind you to see who might be there. After all, it can't possibly be you. But when you turn around, there's nobody there. You look back at the Round Table, and this time the people there are even calling you by your name. Yes. There's no doubt about it. The final place has been reserved for you. You sit down and join the circle, too stunned to say anything.

You're probably wondering what you are doing here. We all do on our first occasion. You see, we were just like you once, no different. All of us, like you, doubted our worthiness. Take a minute of clock time, equal to all the time you need, to ask yourself why the table is round, then the veil that's obscuring the truth will be lifted and everything will become clear to you .....

The truth is that all of us are equal, which is why nobody sits at the head. We all have different strengths and weaknesses and we are all unique. Nobody is better or worse, just different. But all of us share one thing in common. Like you we are part of the Great Mystery, the Oneness that gave birth to us. The time has come for you to claim your rightful place too, the place that is your birthright. So take a minute of clock time, equal to all the time you need, to reconnect with that force …..

If ever you should be plagued by self-doubts again, remember this scene. If ever you should feel isolated, then return to this Table. This chair is always yours.

Now the time has come to return, back to the everyday world waiting for you on the other side. But you return with the recognition of your true worth and this will be with you forever. Never again will you have any cause to doubt your value. So retrace your steps now, back down the aisle, back past the stained glass windows, back, back, through time and actuality, back through the gateway between the two worlds, and back to the place you started from.

Take a deep breath, release it, open your eyes and stretch your arms and legs. Stamp your feet on the ground to make sure you're really back. Welcome home! Take a few minutes in silence to take some notes on the experiences you had on your journeys, which you can then share with the person sitting next to you.

References

Berman, M. (2010) *In A Faraway Land*, Ropley, Hampshire: O-Books.

Eliade, M. (1977) *No Souvenirs: Journal* 1957-1969 San Francisco: Harper & Row Publishers. (Originally published in France as *Fragments d'un Journal* in 1973)

Grinder, J. & Bandler, R. (1981) *Trance Formations*, Utah: Real People Press.

Houston J. (1987) *The Search for the Beloved*, Los Angeles: Tarcher.

McClenon, J., (2002) *Wondrous Healing: Shamanism, Human*

Evolution, and the Origin of Religion, Illinois: Northern Illinois University Press / Dekalb.

Newberg, A., d'Aquili, E., & Rause, V. (2001). *Why God won't go away: Brain science and the biology of belief.* New York: Ballantine.

Nicholoson, S. (ed.) (1987) *Shamanism. An Expanded View of Reality,* Wheaton: The Theosophical Publishing House.

Ruck, Carl A.P., Staples, B.D., Celdran J.A.G., Hoffman, M.A. (2007) *The Hidden World: Survival of Pagan Shamanic Themes in European Fairytales,* North Carolina: Carolina Academic Press.

Shulman, Y.D. (1993) *The Chambers of the Palace: Teachings of Rabbi Nachman of Bratslav,* Northvale, New Jersey: Jason Aronson Inc.

Winkelman, M. (2000) *Shamanism: The Neural Ecology of Consciousness and Healing,* Westport, Connecticut: Bergin & Garvey.

7

Warrior, Settler, or Nomad

Based on the concept of evolutionary psychology, it can be argued that there are three main personality types depending on what we have inherited from our ancestors. The Warrior is forceful, resolute and organisational, the Settler is sociable, intuitive and adaptable, and the Nomad is restless, charismatic and innovative. What kind of learner are you and what are the classroom implications? This chapter will attempt to provide the answers to these questions.

The Warrior needs to be in control and has drive, the ability and desire to manipulate others, speed of thought and the desire to take charge. The Settler is adaptable and able to solve problems, tactful, diplomatic and an effective communicator – often found in caring / nurturing professions. The Nomad is an individual who needs change, drama and excitement. They enjoy feelings of importance and they often spend considerable time attempting to be the centre of attention. We are all predominantly one of these types, as are the learners we work with, and a questionnaire to ascertain your type can be found in the book by Terence Watts listed in the references below.

If you would like to get some idea of the category you fit into, count the number of times the letter 'F' appears in the following sentence:

FINISHED FILES ARE FREQUENTLY
THE RESULT OF YEARS OF
SCIENTIFIC RESEARCH

If you counted correctly the first time, then you are probably a

Warrior type. If you counted correctly the second time you read it, then you are more than likely a Settler, and if you counted incorrectly twice and needed to read it for a third time, then you are probably a Nomad.

When you decide on a course of action, it is important to bear in mind your major personality type and plan accordingly or to access the most appropriate type to give you the resources you need.

The mode in which you automatically think is likely to be the real you whereas the mode in which you behave is probably the result of imprinted behaviour. There is often a conflict between the two and this needs to be resolved before we can function effectively.

One way of developing the other two aspects of your personality can be by making use of affirmations. Affirmations can be described as 'brain convincers' as they can be used to counter the infuriating little voice within which comes with its limiting self-beliefs. They can confuse and contradict our internal belief systems and displace negative and limiting attitudes with more positive ones. A changed image can lead to changed behaviour and this is why affirmations can be such a powerful tool.

Positive reinforcement and carefully chosen words can actually change the structure of the brain. An amine called seratonin plays a critical role. When there is positive reinforcement, seratonin is released simultaneously into the brain and the intestines inducing a sense of well-being and security.

When creating affirmations, there is a golden rule with a very helpful mnemonic device to remind you of it: KISS. It stands for Keep It Simple Stupid. In other words, the affirmations should be phrased as simply and as directly as possible. The subconscious loves simplicity!

Another option available to us is the use of guided visuali-sation and / or self-hypnosis. This entails creating pictures in your mind while following a script. The itinerary of the 'journey' is controlled but the content remains unique to each person taking part in the process. (For an example, see *Taking Your Rightful Place at the Round Table*, in the previous chapter).

In the classroom Warriors are likely to respond to challenges, for Settlers success breeds success so it is important to provide plenty of positive strokes, and Nomads are likely to get bored quickly so will respond favourably to a frequent change of activity. If each lesson you give can provide these three elements, then there is clearly more chance of reaching everyone in the group and of achieving effective results. And now to conclude, there follows a story:

The Three Bees

This is the story of three unfortunate bees whose curiosity got the better of them one sunny day when they fell into an open jam jar.

The first bee wasn't particularly concerned about his predicament because his partner had always rescued him from tricky situations in the past and he trusted that she would do so again. In fact, he'd grown to depend on her. So he just sat back in the jam and waited because he knew that he'd be all right. What happened to him? He died waiting.

The second bee kept climbing the slippery glass wall until he reached the rounded rim, then fell back down again. And the more times he fell, the more determined it made him. He was a fighter and he refused to give in. What happened to him? He died of exhaustion.

The third bee was different to the others and had never really fitted into the hive. In fact, he'd become a social outcast and lived a very solitary life. The other bees had found him to be rather strange and refused to have anything to do with him. Anyway, while his colleagues were otherwise occupied with their own attempts to escape, he chose to taste the jam and what do you know – he found he really liked it. So he ate and he ate and he ate until he'd licked the jar clean. And what happened to him? Well he died too, but he died of pleasure.

Which of the bees was the Nomad, which of the bees was the Settler, and which of the bees was the Warrior? And I wonder which of the bees you would have been – I will leave that for you to answer!

References

Berman M. (2000) *The Power of Metaphor*, Carmarthen: Crown House

Berman M. (2002 2nd Edition) *A Multiple Intelligences Road to an ELT Classroom*, Carmarthen: Crown House

Berman, M. (2008) *Tell us a Story*, Folkestone: Brain Friendly Publications

Watts T. (2000) *Warriors, Settlers & Nomads*, Carmarthen: Crown House

8

Making Use of Divination
in the Classroom

Divination is defined in the Introduction to Loewe and Blacker's *Divination and Oracles* (1981) as 'the attempt to elicit from some higher power or supernatural being the answers to questions beyond the range of ordinary human understanding'. If we concur with the belief that such techniques enable us to catalyze our own unconscious knowledge' (see Von Franz, 1980, p.38), then divination can also be claimed to be the attempt to elicit the answers to such questions from what is commonly referred to in New Age texts as the "inner shaman".

The practice of divination can be traced back into the distant past and by biblical times it was clearly widespread. Despite the warning given to the people of Israel not to follow the "abominable practices" of neighbouring nations, which included human sacrifice, divination, soothsaying, sorcery, mediumship, and necromancy, (see Deuteronomy 18:9-11) we now know that 'Israelite divination corresponded broadly in the range of its uses to the utilisation of divination in Mesopotamia and elsewhere in the Near Eastern environment' (Cryer, 1994, p.324). And there is actually 'no reason to believe that the various phenomena which the Israelites banned as "practices of the peoples" were actually derived from Israel's neighbours' (Cryer, 1994, p.326). Historical linguistics suggests that the forms of magic used in Israel were in all likelihood domestic (see Cryer, 1994, p.262). A good example of this is the goral-lot, for which there is no useful extra-Israelite etymology from the early pre-exilic period. So how come practices forbidden by God were not only utilised by the people of Israel but are also likely to have been domestic rather than the foreign imports they were previously believed to have been by scholars. The answer is simple. 'The strictures against certain types of divination were probably a 'means of restricting the practice to those who were "entitled" to employ it ... to the central cult figures who enjoyed the warrants of power, prestige and, not least, education' (Cryer, 1994, p.327). Cryer's explanation makes perfect sense for if the practice had not been restricted to the chosen few, then the cult figures would no longer have been cult figures and would have had to look for alternative employment.

As Lama Chime Radha Rinpoche points out, one can scarcely expect such a process

> will be totally convincing to someone who has never experienced the reality of divination ... and whose culture conditions him to an almost instinctive and unthinking rejection of everything relating to magic, mystery and the operation of forces and principles which are not at present recognised by modern Western science, [though] ... Jungian psychology, with its concepts of the supra-individual reaches of the unconscious mind, and of intuition as a function of equal validity to that of reason, offers the easiest way for the modern sceptic to arrive at an intellectually respectable position (Loewe & Blacker, 1981, pp.12-13).

It can also be argued that if divination had not been sufficiently successful over the years, it would not still be practised so widely. There remains the possibility, however, that when people are desperate, as a last resort, they are prepared to try anything and that this is the real explanation for its appeal. Clearly more convincing arguments need to be found in order to justify its use.

Kim suggests that 'Instead of trying to rationalize away the irrational nature of shamanism, we need to see that it is precisely its irrationality which gives it its value and its healing power.

Irrationality is important in the field of misfortune, since the experience of misfortune does not really make sense to the sufferer in rational terms' (Kim, 2003, p.224). The same argument could be applied to the use of divination. It would seem to me to be doubtful, however, that experience of misfortune or the results of divination would make any more sense were they to be explained in irrational terms, and that consequently the suggestion is not particularly helpful to our cause. So let us instead consider the "Jungian" position in more depth by turning to the work of one of his followers, the psychotherapist Von Franz.

She points out how the belief that a statistical truth is *the* truth is in fact a fallacy as all we are really handling is an abstract concept, not reality itself. And then goes on to add that if we make the mistake of imagining we are dealing with absolute laws in the field of mathematics, we can then be open to the criticism that we are identifying ourselves with the godhead (see Von Franz, 1980, p.32). On the other hand, people who live on the level of the magic view of the world, such as practitioners of divination, never believe that magic is like an absolute law (see Von Franz, 1980, p.37). Incidentally, nor do they talk about magic in such terms, unless they happen to be unprofessional charlatans.

Von Fanz defines oracle techniques as attempts to get at structures which condition certain psychological probabilities – generally collective patterns of behaviour which lead to us reacting in certain predictable ways in certain situations and she refers to these as archetypes (see Von Fanz, 1980, pp.54&56), and the physicist Wolfgang Pauli thought that by knowing which archetype is being constellated, we can then predict what is likely to follow (see Von Fanz, 1980, p.77). Evidence to support this hypothesis can be seen from the way in which we can have the precognition, without knowing the story, of what will happen next in archetypal stories such as fairy tales (see Von

Franz, 1980, p.79). Whether or not we use the word "archetype" to describe such structures is not particularly important. What we can conclude, however, is that we tend to behave in certain ways when certain circumstances prevail and what diviners do is to refer to these tendencies. And, viewed in this light, the practice of divination surely becomes a lot more acceptable in the eyes of "non-believers".

Let us now go on to consider the part intuition plays in the process. There is a strong likelihood that what we believe to be is our intuition at work is in fact the activation of our unconscious knowledge. 'Our minds process vast amounts of information outside of consciousness, beyond language' (Myers, 2002, p.29) and thoughts, even when they are outside of awareness, clearly influence other thoughts or actions. Consider, for example, what happens when you go shopping for toothpaste and of how, when you reach the shop, a certain brand name comes into your head. The awakening of such associations is known as priming. Unattended stimuli can subtly affect the way we behave in that 'implanted ideas and images can automatically – unintentionally, effortlessly, and without awareness – prime how we interpret and recall events' (Myers, 2002, p.26)

Timothy Wilson argues that the metal processes that control the way we behave are distinct from the mental processes we use to *explain* our behaviour. Often, what seems to happen is that our gut-level attitudes guide our actions, and then our rational mind attempts to make sense of them. From this Wilson concludes that we are often unaware of why we feel the way we do (see Myers, 2002, pp.33-34). We might say, for example we asked for the "Colgate" brand because we know it's good for the teeth, though the real reason could be the effect of the adverts we have seen. 'Reflecting on the reasons for our feelings draws our attention to plausible but possibly erroneous factors' (Myers, 2002, pp.33-34).

Focusing is something people can do *'for themselves and with each other'* (Gendlin, 2003, p.6), something the process shares in common with the technique of "journeying" at least as far as neo-shamanic practitioners are concerned. It has been described 'a process in which you make contact with a special kind of internal bodily awareness' (Gendlin, 2003, p.10) and it is said to be able to profoundly influence our lives and help us reach personal goals. Gendlin claims that 'When your felt sense of a situation changes, *you change* – and therefore, so does your life' (Gendlin, 2003, p.32). The six movements consist of clearing a space, experiencing a felt sense, identifying a handle for it, checking to make sure the felt sense and the word resonate with each other, asking about its qualities, and receiving whatever comes with a shift and staying with it for a while (see Gendlin, 2003, pp.43-45).

Not only is focusing useful as a form of self-help, it can also be adapted for use by learners in other contexts. It can be used to tap into our unconscious storehouse of knowledge when learning a foreign language – when we are unsure of which possibility to opt for in a multiple-choice vocabulary test, for example. We know our passive knowledge of a language is greater than our active use of it and, once we reach a certain level of competence, we are able to tap into that unconscious linguistic sense to find the solutions we seek. The problem is that most of us lack the confidence to take such an apparently illogical approach to the problems of choice we are faced with and so need encouragement and practice in doing so. And once the results are seen to be positive, this fear then naturally disappears.

The suggested way of going about this is, after clearing a space by making use of relaxation techniques, to say each of the possibilities aloud to oneself, and by this process to identify which one feels right, thus tapping into the unconscious storehouse of knowledge. For it is more than likely you will have heard this word or collocation before once you have attained a high level in the language being studied. It has to be pointed out, however, this is less likely to work in the initial stages of studying a language.

What is being proposed here is that effective diviners point out the way in which we tend to behave in certain ways when certain circumstances prevail, and at the same time tap into their vast storehouse of unconscious knowledge. Moreover, it is a technique that, contrary to common belief, all of us, when provided with necessary training, are able to make use of.

References

Cryer, F.H. (1994) *Divination in Ancient Israel and its Near Eastern Environment*, Sheffield: Sheffield Academic Press.

Gendlin, E.T. (2003 25 th Anniversary Edition) *Focusing*, London: Rider (first edition published in 1978).

Loewe, M., & Blacker, C. (eds.) (1981) *Divination and Oracles*, London: George Allen & Unwin Ltd.

Myers, D.G. (2002) *Intuition: Its Powers and Perils*, New Haven and London: Yale University Press.

Von Franz, M.L. (1980) *On Divination and Synchronicity*, Toronto, Canada: Inner City Books.

Wilson, T., Lindsey, S., & Schooler, T.Y. 'A Model of Dual Attitudes,' *Psychological Review 107* (2000) 100-126.

An Aid to CV and Letter Writing
(for Business English Students)

For those learners who are required to write letters in their jobs, the following exercise type has proved to be popular. What it does is to provide them with "skeleton" letters that they can then adapt and modify to suit their own particular requirements. Several examples can be found in *On Business and for Pleasure*, also published by O-Books, and two further samples are presented below:

A letter to find out more information about a product

From each set of alternatives, select the most appropriate choice of wording for a formal letter written to find out more information about a product. Sometimes more than one option might be acceptable, and sometimes perhaps none of them will be:

1.
a. The name, address, and phone number of the person you are writing to on the left hand side of the page.
b. Your name, address, and phone number on the left hand side of the page.
c. The name, address, and phone number of the person you are writing to on the left hand side of the page, followed by your name, address, and phone number.
d. Your name, address, and phone number on the left hand side of the page, followed by the name, address, and phone number of the person you are writing to.

2.

a. Date

b. No date required as it will be on the postmark

3.

a. Dear Mr. _____., Mrs. _____, or Ms. _____,

b. Hello!

c. How are you?

d. Dear Sir/Madam,

e. Esteemed sirs,

f. To whom it may concern:

4.

a. This is a request for information about _____

b. I am interested in _____ that was advertised _____

c. I'd like to know more about _____ what was featured _____

d. I want to know about _____ that I saw advertised _____

e. I would like more information about _____ that was featured _____

f. Please tell me more about _____ what was advertised _____

g. I'm writing because I've got a problem. I need to know more about _____

5.

a. Judging from the advert, the product would seem to be ideal.

b. Based on the information in the advert, the product would suit my needs perfectly.

c. If the advert is to be believed, it seems to be a real bargain.

d. With a bit of luck, it might be just what I've been looking for.

e. I've been trying to get hold of one of these for ages now, so when I saw your advert my eyes nearly popped right out of my head!

6.

a. But I'm still not sure to be honest with you.

b. However, to be honest with you, it all seems a bit too good to be true.

c. But I need to be 100% sure before I go ahead and buy it.

d. However, how can I be sure you're not trying to trick me?

e. But money doesn't grow on trees, you know.

7.

a. That's why I need to know _____

b. For this reason it would be useful if you could tell me _____

c. That is why it would be helpful to know _____

d. So sorry to be a nuisance, but I have to ask _____

e. So don't give me any bullshit and just tell me straight:_____?

8.

a. It would also be helpful if you could tell me _____

b. One more thing I need to know is _____

c. It would also be appreciated if you could tell me _____

d. Another thing I need to know is _____

e. It would also be helpful if you could let me know _____

9.

a. And last but not least, details of _____ would be a help too.

b. Finally, and perhaps most important of all, we also need to know _____

c. And one more thing too, before it slips my mind. I want to know _____

d. Additionally, some more details about _____ would assist us enormously too.

10.

a. If I don't report back with this information quickly, my boss is going to murder me so please don't let me down.

b. I would be grateful if you could provide me with this information as soon as possible please.

c. Thank you in advance for your cooperation.

d. Thanks a lot for helping me out.

e. Please answer this quickly and don't mess me around.

f. A quick response would be very much appreciated as time is of the essence.

g. A quick response would be very much appreciated as I'm a busy man and don't take kindly to being made to wait for things.

11.

a. Sincerely,

b. Yours sincerely

c. Faithfully,

d. Yours faithfully,

e. Your obedient servant

f. With all good wishes

g. I remain, as always, yours truly

h. All the best,

12.

a. PS 'Sorry about the recycled envelope, but I didn't have any new ones left and all the shops were closed.

b. I would like to apologize for posting this to you in a recycled envelope. Unfortunately, due to an administrative error, we ran out of new ones and, under the circumstances, it was the only way to ensure the letter reached you quickly.

c. PS. 'Sorry about the recycled envelope, but we're into saving trees in our office – one of my boss's bright ideas!

SUGGESTED ANSWERS: 1b / 2a / 3a and 3d / 4b and 4e / 5a and 5b / 6b / 7b and 7c / 8a and 8c and 8e / 9b and 9d / 10b / 11b and 11d (use 11b if the person is referred to by name at the start of the letter) 12 All three options would be inappropriate

A letter offering an apology

From each set of alternatives, select the most appropriate choice of wording for a formal letter written to find out more information about a product. Sometimes more than one option might be acceptable, and sometimes perhaps none of them will be:

1.
a. The name, address, and phone number of the person you are writing to on the left hand side of the page.
b. Your name, address, and phone number on the left hand side of the page.
c. The name, address, and phone number of the person you are writing to on the left hand side of the page, followed by your name, address, and phone number.
d. Your name, address, and phone number on the left hand side of the page, followed by the name, address, and phone number of the person you are writing to.

2.
a. Date
b. No date required as it will be on the postmark

3.
a. Dear Mr. _____., Mrs. _____, or Ms. _____,
b. Hello!
c. How are you?
d. Dear Sir/Madam,
e. Esteemed sirs,

f. To whom it may concern:

4.

a. Pursuant to your letter of _____
b. Regarding your letter dated _____
c. In response to your letter of _____
d. About the letter you sent me dated _____

5.

a. I would first of all like to say how sorry we were to hear of your concerns.
b. all I can say is that it wasn't my fault
c. I was of course most upset to learn of the problems you have experienced
d. I'm really sorry about what's happened and wuill do my best to sort out the mess.
e. You must be mad to think I'm going to accept responsibility for what's happened.
f. We would first of all like to offer you our sincere apologies for what has unfortunately taken place.

6.

a. I can assure you that we take such matters very seriously,
b. To be honest with you, we get letters like this all the time and just bin them.
c. We will of course carry out a full investigation into what has taken place.
d. And you have every right to feel pissed off about the way you've been treated
e. If it had happened to me, I'd have been furious too.

7.

a. But it takes two to make a quarrel, and you need to accept that you're partly to blame too.

b. However, according to our records, we cannot be held entirely responsible for what has transpired.

c. However, based on the information you originally provided us with, we did our best, and would like to point out that the majority of our customers are more than happy with what we provide.

8.

a. Nevertheless, in view of the inconvenience you have undoubtedly suffered, I have enclosed a cheque to cover the extra costs you have incurred.

b. Nonetheless, to compensate you for the trouble you have experienced, enclosed please find a cheque to cover the extra costs you have had.

c. Anyway, regardless of whose fault it is, I'm enclosing a cheque to cover the extra costs you say you've had.

d. In any case, even tough you've been a real pain in the backside, attached to this letter you'll find a cheque which should help to shut you up

9.

a. Trusting this will meet with your approval,

b. So hope you'll let the matter drop now.

c. And I hope I never hear from you again.

d. I hope you find this acceptable.

e. I hope this is acceptable to you.

10.

a. Sincerely,

b. Yours sincerely,

c. Faithfully,

d. Yours faithfully,

e. Your obedient servant

f. With all good wishes

g. I remain, as always, yours truly

h. All the best,

SUGGESTED ANSWERS: 1b / 2a / 3a and 3d / 4b and 4c / 5a and 5c and 5e / 6a and 6c / 7b and 7c / 8a and 8b / 9d and 9e / 10b (if the person is referred to by name at the start of the letter) or 10d (if no name is given)

Now for those learners who need help to produce CVs in English, here's some advice on how to produce the perfect one, which is presented in the form of a gap-fill activity.

Find the missing words in the following text:

The recruiter who receives your CV will probably have loads to sort through and very little time in which to do the job, so your CV will have to showcase your relevant experience, skills and qualities as succinctly as possible. Simplification is the 1 _____ to success.

STRUCTURE YOUR CV.
The most important information should be clearly 2 _____ out at the very beginning of your CV, as it's this that will get you long-listed for an interview. Don't 3 _____ the recruiter will search through reams of information to find out if you're qualified for a position – they won't!

KEEP IT SHORT
Whilst there's no 4 _____ and fast rule for the length of a CV, a couple of pages are usually 5 _____ as the norm. Keep it punchy, get your 6 _____ in the door and 7 _____ the more involved explanations for your interview.

KEEP IT SWEET

Your CV should not become a confessional, a list of mishaps or a series of excuses. Exorcise any references to failure – 8 _____ that's examination, marital or business. Instead, write positively and 9 _____ your best face to the world.

MAKE IT LOOK GOOD

Decorative patterns and eccentric formatting can often 10 _____ from your message. Keep your CV uncluttered with short sentences, big margins around your text and key points emphasised. Bullet 11 _____ can be useful, but in moderation.

TAILOR YOUR CV

A 12 _____ -fire way to boost your chances of getting an interview is to tweak your CV for each application you make. So go through the job spec with a fine tooth 13 _____, making sure to include examples proving relevant experience for all requirements of the role.

DON'T LEAVE SUSPICIOUS GAPS

Any unexplained gap in your employment history will create suspicion, so make sure to 14 _____ those holes. Even times of unemployment can be adequately 15 _____ if you focus on the development of soft skills such as project management, communication or teamwork.

CHECK, CHECK, CHECK. AND THEN CHECK AGAIN

Any spelling or grammatical mistakes in your CV are going to create a negative 16 _____ in the 17 _____ of the recruiter – why would they want to employ someone slapdash? Spell-checkers can often 18 _____ up erroneously altering words to American spelling conventions so don't rely on them. Instead, ask people you can trust to go over your CV for typos and grammatical errors.

DITCH THE SNAPSHOT AND PERSONAL INFO.

Unless specifically asked to provide a photo of yourself, 19 _____ it out. The skills, achievements and experience you describe should 20 _____ weight with the recruiter, not your hairstyle or any other personal information unless strictly 21 _____ to your application.

BE HONEST

Never, ever 22 _____ the truth in your job application, no 23 _____ how well you think you can 24 _____ it up, for sooner of later you will be found out. So by all 25 _____ highlight the positives in your CV, but don't include blatant lies – even in the section on your leisure activities.

ANSWERS: 1 key / 2 laid / 3 assume / 4 hard / 5 regarded / 6 foot / 7 save / 8 whether / 9 present / 10 detract / 11 points / 12 sure / 13 comb / 14 plug / 15 justified / 16 perception / 17 mind / 18 end / 19 leave / 20 carry / 21 relevant / 22 embellish / 23 matter / 24 cover / 25 means

And finally, for those students uncertain as to what sort of job might be right for them, perhaps this exercise might prove to be useful:

The right job for the right person

Choose the best answer form each pair of alternatives. In most cases, only one of the answers is correct, but sometimes they both might be suitable. So be careful!

To 1. say / tell you 2. a / the truth, I would not 3. want / wish to be in your 4. boots / shoes for all the tea in 5. China / India. In 6. first place / the first place, I am just not cut 7. out / up for a managerial role. I wouldn't be able to 8. cope / face with all the responsibilities such a position 9. entails / involves. 10. What is more / Moreover, I am sure I would 11. do / make a complete mess of it. So appointing me would just be asking for 12. trouble / troubles, and nobody in their right 13. brain / mind would even consider 14. doing / to do so. You'd be much better off 15. giving / to give the job to someone else and 16. allowing / letting me to concentrate instead on what I do best, 17. that / which is 18. dealing / managing with 19. a / the general public. After all, I've been doing it for years and, as you should know by now, you can be sure I won't 20. get / let you down.

Now for something you can do with a friend, a colleague, or in class with a teacher. What kind of job would suit you – one that involves a lot of overseas travel, one in which you can use your language skills, one which offers the prospect of promotion, one that required good interpersonal skills, one that would enable you to work in a caring profession, one that would enable you to use your initiative, one that would provide you with security for life, one in which you can be your own boss, one you can do from home, one which involves taking risks, one that would provide you with a regular income, one in which all you have to do is to follow orders, one that would provide you with plenty of variety, or one that would give you more free time?

Select three of the options or, if none of them suit you, produce three of your own. Then be prepared to justify the choices you make to the person sitting next to you. After that you will have the opportunity to tell the rest of the class what you found out.

ANSWERS: 1 tell 2 the 3 want / wish 4 shoes 5 China 6 the first place 7 out 8 cope 9 entails / involves 10 What is more / Moreover 11 make 12 trouble 13 mind 14 doing 15 giving 16 allowing 17 which 18 dealing 19 the 20 let

10

Teaching Idioms

Whenever you ask higher level students what they would like to do more work on, the answer is invariably idioms, and phrasal verbs in particular. What is an idiom and why do they cause so many problems for students? An idiom can be defined as a phrase which has a different meaning from the meaning of its separate components. One of the characteristics of idioms is that you cannot normally change the words, their order, or the grammatical forms in the same way as you can change non-idiomatic expression. In other words, idioms are basically fixed expressions.

Sometimes the meaning of the idioms can be guessed from the meaning of one of the words but usually the meaning is completely different, which is why they are so tricky for students.

Care needs to be taken when writing idioms as many of them are only used in informal language. On the other hand, there are other expressions that are literary or old-fashioned and unsuitable for use in everyday language, except perhaps as a joke.

Grouping idioms according to topic can not only make them easier for students to learn. It also make it easier for teachers to relate the exercises to topic-based units in course books and the following matching activities were designed with these aims in mind. As a follow-up, you can arrange the students in groups and invite them to write dialogues incorporating as many of the idioms as they can. This can even be made into a competition, with a prize being awarded to the group who manage to include the highest number.

***

MOUTH IDIOMS: Match the idioms with the explanations like the example in bold type. There are more explanations than you need so make sure you select the right ones!

1. You took the words right out of my mouth.
2. The trouble with you is that you're all mouth and trousers.
3. Why are you so down in the mouth today?
4. I was born with a silver spoon in my mouth.
5. I had my heart in my mouth.
6. It left a nasty taste in my mouth.
7. **It made my mouth water.**
8. Stop putting words in my mouth.
9. Since moving to London, I've been living from hand to mouth.
10. You look as if butter wouldn't melt in your mouth.

a. I felt anxious.
b. **I felt hungry.**
c. I felt passionate.
d. I felt thirsty.
e. It created a bad impression.
f. It gave me an upset stomach.
g. I was born into a rich family.
h. I was born with a speech impediment.
i. Life has been a struggle.
j. Life has been easy.
k. Somehow you knew what I was going to say.
l. Stop misquoting me.
m. Support your words with actions.
n. You're all talk and no action, aren't you?
o. You're not a harmless as you seem to be, are you?
p. You're ruled by your heart, not your head.
q. You're very miserable, aren't you?

1 ___ 2 ___ 3 ___ 4 ___ 5 ___ 6 ___ 7 **b** 8 ___ 9 ___ 10 ___

ANSWERS: 1-k 2-n 3-q 4-g 5-a 6-e 7-b 8-l 9-i 10-o

HEAVEN AND HELL IDIOMS: Match the idioms on the left with the explanations on the right. There are more explanations than you need so make sure you select the correct ones!

1. Living with you is heaven on earth.

a. Having good intentions isn't enough.

2. I'd move heaven and earth to get that job.

b. I'm not going to let anything stand in my way.

3. I'm determined to succeed come hell or high water.

c. I don't care what happens to you.

4. As far as I'm concerned, you can go to hell.

d. I think you've got a really good chance.

5. You haven't got a hope in hell.

e. It's going to cost a great deal of money.

6. The road to hell is paved with good intentions.

f. Living with you is everything I've always wanted.

7. I'm afraid there's going to be hell to pay!

g. Living with you is unbearable

8. You scared the hell out of me.

h. There's going to be a lot of trouble.

9. What you're asking for is pennies from heaven.

i. Whatever happens, I won't give up.

j. What you're asking for is a miracle.

k. What you're doing is begging.

l. You gave me an awful fright.

m. You've got no chance at all.

n. You helped me to overcome my fear.

ANSWERS: 1-f 2-b 3-i 4-c 5-m 6-a 7-h 8-l 9-j

BLACK AND WHITE IDIOMS: Match the idioms with the explanations like the example in bold type. There are more explanations than you need so make sure you select the right ones!

1. I want your promise in black and white.
2. Why are you giving me such black looks?
3. **Why do you always look on the black side?**
4. You're the kind of person who'll swear black is white to get what you want!
5. I'm not as black as I'm painted.
6. I'm the black sheep of my family.
7. It's time you waved the white flag.
8. You're bleeding me white and I can't take any more!
9. It was only a white lie so I hope you'll forgive me.
10. Thankfully I'm now in the black again.

a. **Don't be so pessimistic!**
b. Fortunately I'm no longer in debt.
c. I'm different to all the rest and they disapprove of me.

d. I'm happy to say that I've found another job and I'm no longer unemployed.

e. I'm not as bad as people say.

f. I didn't tell you the truth but for a good reason.

g. I think you'd better admit defeat.

h. It's time you stood up for yourself.

i. Please put it in writing.

j. What on earth have I done to upset you?

k. Why are you always criticising me?

l. You're constantly insulting me and I've had enough.

m. You're making me spend all my money on you.

n. You're prepared to use any means possible to achieve your ends.

1 ___ 2 ___ **3 a** 4 ___ 5 ___ 6 ___ 7 ___ 8 ___ 9 ___ 10 ___

ANSWERS: 1-i 2-j 3-a 4-n 5-e 6-c 7-g 8-m 9-f 10-b

The Room Full of Books and Your Students' Writing: How to Improve it

His room was full of books – books of all shapes, sizes and descriptions – books that had been read and re-read, annotated and dog-marked, books containing slips of paper with added handwritten notes inserted into their covers, and books which had key pages marked with paperclips. They were all neatly arranged alphabetically and in order of size. Nobody was allowed to touch them without his permission and woe betide anyone who broke that rule. The daily help who'd made the mistake of trying to dust them was instantaneously dismissed and a torrent of abuse was hurled at her, the likes of which she'd never encountered before. Unbeknown to the old fellow, she'd formerly worked in a massage parlour, but not even her clients had ever talked to her like that. One could only wonder where the old man had learnt such language. Surely not from the few private patients he still saw once a week in his Harley Street practice.

It was these books that had formed the starting point for his own writing. And very impressive his writing was too – indicative of the broad range of disciplines he'd obtained qualifications in over the years. Not only was he an allopathic doctor, but he also had qualifications in homoeopathy, and was a fellow of the Royal College of Psychiatrists. Moreover, though now well into his eighties, he was more determined than ever not to let his mind rot, and had recently taken up the study of Chinese herbal medicine to add to his considerable list of achievements.

Shut away in his library, he'd long since lost touch with the concerns that affected his patients and had long since lost any ability to empathize with what they were going through. He simply used his considerable powers of persuasion to convince them that his way was the only one. His reputation preceded him and no one dared to question his pronouncements.

The old boy was not short of disciples – they would come from far and wide to visit him and tap into his undoubted wisdom. He was not the sort of person to suffer fools gladly and most of them were given short shrift. However, there was one he was particularly fond of who stood out from all the rest. His name was Frank. There was something about the young student that reminded him of the kind of person he'd once been. He greatly looked forward to Frank's weekly visits as his questions helped to keep him on his toes.

However, one week Frank just stopped coming. The master was thrown by this at first but quickly found an explanation for the untoward behaviour shown by his most promising protégé. "You see," he told an audience of the new recruits one day, "the time had come for Frank to move on as you all will one day too." Of course he never bothered to check out his theory. He didn't have to as he had all the answers in his books.

And the real explanation for Frank's disappearance? There had been a nagging doubt in Frank's mind for some time – one that grew slowly but surely. And the more time he spent in the company of the master, the more disillusioned he had become. "What is the true definition of wisdom? If this man I look up to is indeed so wise, why is it that he can't hear the responses to the questions he asks me? Why is it that I get the feeling that nothing I say registers with him, and that all he is looking for in me is confirmation of his own theories?" But Frank knew there was absolutely no point in confronting the old boy with these facts. He was too far gone and he'd wasted enough time on him as it was.

Frank was, however, eternally grateful for the one lesson of value he had learnt from the many hours he had spent together with the old man – how not to behave. True wisdom comes from listening, not for confirmation of the theories found in books, but for the exceptions that disprove them.

In small groups, work through the following questions, and then elect a spokesperson to present you answers to the rest of the class:

    a. How many books are there in the room where you live, and what kind are they?

    b. Is there a book you have read or a film you have seen that has significantly changed your life in some way?

    c. Do you know anybody like the old man in the story or like Frank, his disciple?

    d. What do you consider the mark of true wisdom to be?

    e. "Read and re-read, annotated and dog-marked ..." What other adjectives can be used to describe books? Make a list of them.

    f. Having read this story, do you think it has changed your attitude towards the knowledge to be gained from books in any way?

ABUSE is an uncountable noun in English, which means it cannot be used with indefinite article, though we can say *a torrent of abuse.*

Now match the words below on the left with the uncountable nouns on the right:

a torrent of	a. air or electricity
stream of	b. blood or molten lava
oceans of	c. consciousness
a puddle of	d. conversation or information
a current of	e. criticism
a pool of	f. inspiration
a source of	g. light
a flow of	h. rainwater
rivers of	i. space

The Room Full of Books

Level: Upper Intermediate to Advanced
Target Audience: Adults
Language / Skills Focus: Listening, Speaking, and Uncountable Nouns
Materials: Photocopies of the story / worksheet to hand out after the storytelling.

IN CLASS

Pre-listening: Who would you turn to first if you were ill, and why – an allopathic or a homoeopathic doctor? This story is about a man who was qualified in both forms of medicine.

While-listening: Find out what other qualifications that the old man had, and the former occupation of his daily help.

Post-listening: Hand out the photocopies. Ask the learners to work through the activities under the story individually, and then to compare their answers in pairs or small groups.

Find words in the story which mean the same as: a. woe betide anyone / b. instantaneously dismissed / c. not to let his mind rot / d. empathize with what they were going through / e. His reputation preceded him / f. no one dared to question his pronouncements / g. not the sort of person to suffer food gladly / h. to keep him on his toes / i. too far gone
Match the words on the left with the uncountable nouns on the right: 1-e / 2-c / 3-i / 4-h / 5-a / 6-g / 7-f / 8-d / 9-b

COMMENTS
This contemporary short story can be used as a lead-in to a discussion on reading habits, and / or the value of the

knowledge that can be obtained from books. It can also provide a springboard into a discussion on alternative forms of medicine. As a follow-up to the story, the check list provided below could be handed out to the learners - something I prepared for a mixed nationality Cambridge Proficiency class I was teaching after I received their first written assignments. It was clear that despite their different backgrounds, there were problems they had in common that needed to be addressed and this list was produced in an attempt to help them. I have since used it with other classes preparing for exams, adapting it to suit their particular problems and needs, and you might like to do the same with it:

Your written English: how to improve it

Check through your work before you submit it for the mistakes you know you have a tendency to make. For example, if you are a Polish, Japanese, or a Turkish speaker, it is likely you have problems in using the articles "a" and "the", because you do not have them in your languages.

If you have written a particularly long sentence, check it for punctuation, and also to make sure you have used appropriate connectors.

If the requirement is to produce a formal piece of writing, then do not use contracted forms.

Remember to include third person S for verbs in the Present Simple, preceded by "he", "she" or "it", or their equivalents.

Avoid repetition. If you have used a word once, try to use a synonym for it or an alternative when you refer to it again.

Try to upgrade the vocabulary you use. For example, there is always a more impressive adjective you can use in place of "nice", and there are many alternatives to "very" – "extremely" or "incredibly", for example. Take the opportunity to show the examiner just how much you know.

Focus on quality, not quantity. There is no point in writing twice as much as everyone else if all it shows the examiner is that your English is not up to the standard required.

Do not be frightened to make mistakes at this stage - just make sure that you learn from them. After all, it is better to make them now than in the exam. Now is a time for experimenting, but the exam is a time to play safe and to stick to what you are sure of.

Do not use idioms unless you are sure they are correct. There is nothing more noticeable than an idiom misused – it will stick out like a sore thumb.

Use certain structures in moderation. For example, an inversion after a negative adverb will impress the examiner, but not if you try to include one in every single sentence you write.

Pay particular attention to your opening sentence and your conclusion, as the examiner will probably look more closely at these, and the opening will clearly colour the initial impression he / she forms of your work.

Do not attempt to write you assignment twice as you will certainly not have time to do so in the exam. Take some initial notes if you like, but then write the actual assignment once only or you will find you run out of time.

If your handwriting is difficult to read, then consider only writing on every other line so have more space to make corrections in.

Remember if you wish to add a missing word, the sign for it in English is an inverted letter V placed below the line.

Also make sure you know how to use inverted commas for title in English as they come above the line, both before and after the name of the film or the book. For example, "War and Peace".

The longer your sentences are, the more danger there is of making mistakes. However, writing too many short sentences that contain only one idea will not create a good impression either. What you need is to find a balance between the two extremes.

***

A problematic area for advanced level learners is the use of collocations with adverbs and adjectives, and one course books tend to neglect. So here are a couple of exercises to help your students both to activate their passive knowledge and to upgrade the level of vocabulary they make use of in their work:

Collocations with adverbs & adjectives (i)

Match the adverbs with the sets of adjectives. Use each adverb once only. Then use some of the collocations to fill in the gaps in the sentences:

1 completely 2 deeply 3 fiercely 4 greatly 5 heavily 6 highly 7 keenly 8 poorly 9 readily 10 richly 11 severely 12 tastefully 13 seriously

a. accepted / agreed / available
b. acclaimed / desirable / overrated
c. adorned / deserved / illustrated
d. appreciated / relieved / respected
e. committed / injured / flawed
f. competitive / independent / proud
g. concerned / disturbed / religiou
h. contested / disputed / fought
i. criticised / disabled / incapacitated
j. decorated / dressed / furnished
k. equipped / finished / presented
l. exhausted / outplayed / unacceptable
m. involved / pregnant / sedated

1. The system currently in use is seriously _____ and in need of an urgent overhaul.

2. I admit that the product is cheaper than ours, but the truth is that it is poorly _____ and is clearly not built to last.

3. In view of the recession, the pay cut was readily _____ to by staff and management alike. .

4. All the overtime I have been obliged to do recently has left me feeling completely _____

5. Having been heavily _____ in the project since the outset, we were not surprisingly extremely disappointed when it was decided to pull the plug on it.

6. The industrial accident left the employee severely _____ and unable to work any more.

7. Our latest catalogue has not only been printed on glossy paper but is also richly _____ and has been produced with no expense spared.

8. I am deeply _____ about the effect our latest product is having on the environment and, as a result, I have grave doubts about whether I really want to represent this company any more.

9. Being fiercely _____ is not a bad thing as long as you keep it within reasonable limits and do not let it take control of your life to the exclusion of everything else.

10. We were severely _____ for the poor quality of our presentation and the truth is we probably deserved it.

11. As she leads by example, she is greatly _____ by all her staff and they are one hundred per cent loyal to her.

12. It was a keenly _____ election and I was lucky to get re-appointed on to the committee. To tell you the truth, I didn't think I was going to make it this time.

ANSWERS: 1-l / 2-g / 3-f / 4-d / 5-m / 6-b / 7-h / 8-k / 9-a / 10-c / 11-i / 12-j / 13-e

1 flawed 2 finished 3 agreed 4 exhausted 5 involved 6 disturbed

7 illustrated 8 concerned 9 competitive 10 criticised 11 respected 12 fought

**

Collocations with adverbs & adjectives (ii)

Match the adverbs with the sets of adjectives. Use each adverb once only. Then use some of the collocations to fill in the gaps in the sentences:

1 abundantly 2 acutely 3 bitterly 4 completely 5 conveniently 6 dreadfully 7 highly 8 severely 9 strictly 10 fatally 11 hopelessly 12 hotly 13 ridiculously 14 utterly

a. aware / conscious / painful
b. clear / documented / obvious
c. cold / divided / opposed
d. confused / ineffective / lost
e. contested / denied / pursued
f. depressed / limited / reduced
g. easy / expensive / overdressed
h. fed up / ridiculous / unsuitable
i. flawed / injured / underestimated
j. forbidden / platonic / true
k. forgotten / ignored / situated
l. hopeless / lost / unreasonable
m. influential / unlikely / valued
n. sorry / tired / upset

1. I hope I have made it abundantly _____ by now that I wish to have nothing more to do with you.
2. Though she is obviously an extremely attractive woman, our relationship is strictly _____ and will remain that way.

3. I am dreadfully _____ if I upset you and want you to know that it was never my intention to do so.

4. Though you have been bitterly _____ to the plan since the outset, you have never once come up with any form of alternative.

5. What we can do in the way of promoting the product is severely _____ due to financial constraints.

6. You seem to have conveniently _____ all the promises you made when you first started working for us.

7. All the new rules and regulations that have been introduced have left me hopelessly _____ and I am no longer sure what we can or cannot do any more.

8. Though he hotly _____ having attempted to mislead us, I still felt he was not being entirely honest and was not convinced.

9. What you wore to the interview was so completely _____ that it is no wonder you failed to impress.

10. There is no need to remind me because I am acutely _____ of the problem. In fact, it is all I ever think abut these days.

11. You fatally _____ the opposition and you paid the price. I only hope now you can learn from what has happened so that you never make the same mistake again.

12. It seems to be such a ridiculously _____ way of making money that there must surely be some kind of catch to it. You'd better read the small print again to make sure you have not misunderstood anything before you go ahead and invest in it.

13. It is utterly _____ of you to expect me to take on all these extra responsibilities when I already have so much work to do.

14. As a highly _____ client of ours, we would like to reward you in some way for your loyalty over the years by offering you this exclusive deal.

ANSWERS: 1-b / 2-a / 3-c / 4-h / 5-k / 6-n / 7-m / 8-f / 9-j / 10-i / 11-d / 12-e / 13-g / 14-l

1 clear 2 platonic 3 sorry 4 opposed 5 limited 6 forgotten 7 confused 8 denied 9 unsuitable 10 aware 11 underestimated 12 easy 13 unsuitable 14 valued

Finally, an activity to help those learners (in other words, more or less all students and many native speakers too) who have problems when it comes to using commas:

Vegetarianism and how to punctuate it!

Working in pairs or small groups, decide which of these sentences need commas inserted into them, where they should be placed, and why:

    a. If you're a vegetarian you don't eat meat or fish.

    b. You don't eat meat or fish if you're a vegetarian.

    c. I'm a vegetarian. I eat fish sometimes though.

    d. I'm a vegetarian who sometimes eats fish.

    e. I'm a vegetarian which means I never eat meat or fish.

    f. I'm a vegetarian. However I sometimes eat fish.

    g. I'm a vegetarian. Moreover I'm a teetotaller.

    h. Being a vegetarian I never eat meat or fish.

    i. In my opinion meat-eaters are murderers.

j. I don't eat meat because I've found that it makes me nervous.

ANSWERS: a. A comma is required after an IF clause in front position in a sentence b. No comma is used when the IF clause comes second in a sentence c. A comma is required before THOUGH d. No comma is used before a defining clause e. A comma is required before a non-defining clause f. A comma is required after the connector HOWEVER in front position g. A comma is required after the connector MOREOVER in front position h. A comma is required after a participle clause i. A comma is required after the sentence opener IN MY OPINION j. No comma is used before BECAUSE

12

The Implications of
Multiple Intelligences Theory

IQ Tests were developed by Binet early in the 20th century and were frequently used to assess the potential of children in schools until quite recently. Tests of this type, however, have now fallen into disrepute. All they test is linguistic and logical-mathematical intelligence and this traditional definition of intelligence is now regarded as too narrow. We now know that 75% of teachers are sequential, analytical presenters but 70% of students do not actually learn this way! The educational psychologist most responsible for this change of attitude is Howard Gardner, the creator of the Multiple Intelligence Theory.

In 1983 Gardner suggested that all individuals have personal intelligence profiles that consist of combinations of seven different intelligence types. These intelligences are (Gardner 1983, 1993): verbal-linguistic / logical-mathematical / visual-spatial / bodily-kinaesthetic / musical-rhythmic / intrapersonal / interpersonal Gardner later added an eighth intelligence type to the list, that of naturalist intelligence. At the same time he suggested the existence of a ninth intelligence type, that of existentialist intelligence (Gardner 1999).

Gardner refers to Intelligences as potentials that will or will not be activated, depending upon the values of a particular culture, the opportunities available in that culture, and the personal decisions made by individuals and/or their families, schoolteachers, and others.

A student who believes that intelligence can be developed is likely to be persistent and adventurous. However, a learner who thinks that ability is fixed, is more likely to get upset when faced with failure as it can only be construed as evidence of inadequate ability. The fluid 'theory' of intelligence advocated by Gardner encourages students to stretch themselves.

In his book *Intelligence Reframed* Gardner adds Naturalist Intelligence, our talent for classifying and categorising, to the original Magnificent Seven. He also speculates on the possibility of their being both a spiritual intelligence and an existential intelligence but comes to no definite conclusions. When discussing the existence of a ninth intelligence type, existentialist intelligence, Gardner also used an alternative term, spiritual intelligence.

Existentialist learners need to see "the big picture" in order to understand minor parts and details. One of the best ways for foreign-language teachers to cater for this type of intelligence is therefore to start each lesson by introducing the teaching goals and by telling their students where the linguistic input of the present lesson (whether related to themes or grammar points) fits in with the linguistic input of previous taught lessons, i.e. in relation to a larger context. Suitable reading and discussion exercises for existentialist learners can often be found in books that focus on the use of metaphors in order to stimulate the readers' imagination and feelings –Useful titles written especially for foreign-language teaching purposes are *The Power of Metaphor - Story Telling & Guided Journeys for Teachers, Trainers and Therapists* (Berman & Brown 2000) and *In a Faraway Land* (Berman 2010).

According to Danah Zohar, author of *Spiritual Intelligence The Ultimate Intelligence,* SQ (Spiritual Intelligence) is what we use to develop our longing and capacity for meaning, vision and value. It facilitates a dialogue between reason and emotion, between mind and body. SQ allows us to integrate the intrapersonal and the interpersonal, to transcend the gap between self and other.

There is believed to be a built-in spiritual centre located among neural connections in the temporal lobes of the brain. On scans taken with positron emission topography these neural areas light up whenever research subjects are exposed to discussion of spiritual or religious topics. Neurobiologists have now dubbed the area of the temporal lobes concerned with religious or spiritual experience the 'God spot' or the 'God module'.

The brain's unitive experience emanates from synchronous 40 Hz neural oscillations that travel across the whole brain. According to Zohar, the 40 Hz oscillations are the neural basis of SQ, a third intelligence that places our actions and experience in a larger context of meaning and value, thus rendering them more effective. Everything possesses a degree of proto-consciousness but only certain special structures, like brains, have what is needed to generate full-blown consciousness. In this case, we conscious human beings have our roots at the origin of the universe itself. Our spiritual intelligence grounds us in the wider cosmos, and life has purpose and meaning within the larger context of cosmic evolutionary processes.

As well as there being a case for adding Spiritual Intelligence to Gardner's list, it can also be argued that there is a Metaphoric Intelligence. Dr Jeannette Littlemore, in *Humanizing Language Teaching* (2001a), makes a case for there being a 'Metaphoric Intelligence' (an ability to comprehend and produce novel metaphors) and suggests that this might bring a number of benefits to the language learning process. She claims to provide theoretical and empirical evidence showing that metaphoric intelligence does indeed meet Gardner's eight criteria for the existence of an intelligence type. However, Gardner himself makes no mention of Metaphoric Intelligence and it is still open to debate whether it exists or not. Moreover, a case can be made for what has been called metaphoric Intelligence having points in common with Zohar's 'Spiritual Intelligence', such as an ability to see a connection between diverse phenomena. Whether we view metaphoric intelligence as an acquired skill, or as a distinct intelligence, the fact remains that it is likely to have a number of useful applications in language learning. It should enrich language production and facilitate the comprehension of metaphoric expressions. It is therefore likely to contribute positively to an overall level of communicative competence.

All individuals have personal intelligence profiles that consist of combinations of different intelligence types. It is not, however, so much a matter of either possessing or not possessing specific intelligence types. Even if a specific type of intelligence may in theory be non-existent in some individuals, the large majority of us do have at least a minimal degree of all intelligence types. According to Mary Ann Christison (2005), most people are somewhere in the middle of the scale, with a few intelligences highly developed, most modestly developed, and one or two underdeveloped.

It is important to note, however, that people's MI profiles are not static. Unlike traditional IQ, intelligence as defined by Gardner (1999) in his MI theory, can – and does – change. This means that the nine intelligence types can develop, and also be developed.

Depending on their personal MI profiles, people tend to develop their own favourite way (or ways) of learning foreign languages. For vocabulary learning, for example, some prefer traditional rote learning. Others divide the foreign words into parts or components and concentrate on memorising these instead. Some look for similarities between the foreign-language words and grammatical structures and the corresponding words and structures in their mother tongue or other languages they may know. Some people find mnemonic devices helpful, at least occasionally. Others have adopted different types of accelerated learning techniques and use them on a more or less permanent basis.

Does the fact that we each have a unique profile mean that we should plan individual lessons for everyone in the class to take this into account? Clearly this would be impractical and the solution lies in including material designed to appeal to each of the types in every lesson we give. The table presented below lists classroom activities that cater for the different Intelligence types. However, this classification is clearly subjective and dependent on individual teaching styles. Moreover, it should also be pointed out that a number of the activities cater for more than one Intelligence type and could consequently be placed in more than one category:

Activities to develop the intelligences

Linguistic Intelligence: group discussions and organized debates / reading / storytelling / completing worksheets / word building games / giving presentations and reports / producing summaries / listening to lectures.

Logical-mathematical Intelligence: logic puzzles / problem solving activities / logical-sequential presentations / guided discovery / ordering, matching and gap fill activities / utilizing statistics to develop arguments / cultural comparisons and contrasts.

Visual/Spatial Intelligence: charts / graphs and diagrams / mind maps / peripherals / videos / illustrating concepts and things / reading maps and interpreting directions.

Bodily-kinaesthetic Intelligence: Circle Dancing / Relaxation Exercises / Brain Gym / Craftwork / Flashcards / acting out an event or thing / cooperative or competitive games.

Musical Intelligence: Songs / Background Music / Jazz Chants / creating songs or jingles.

Interpersonal Intelligence: Circle Time / group work / paired activities / brainstorming / peer teaching / questionnaires, surveys and polls / board games / interactive software programmes / team problem solving / simulations / group writing projects.

Intrapersonal Intelligence: project work / independent study and individual instruction / monitoring of own skills / researching and online activities / essay writing / learner diaries / personal goal setting / reflective learning activities.

Naturalist Intelligence: classifying & categorizing activities / hands-on learning / nature walks or field trips.

Spiritual Intelligence: guided visualisation / storytelling / promoting reflective learning by asking 'Why?' or 'What if?' questions.

Metaphoric intelligence: the use of extended metaphors in debates / guesswork / 'think aloud' activities where the learners work out the meanings of metaphors together

It is clear that unless we teach multi-modally and cater for all the intelligence types in each of our lessons, we will fail to reach all the learners in the group whichever approach to teaching we adopt. Another reason for teaching multi-modally is that with high levels of stimulus and challenge there are higher ratios of synapses (connections) to the neurons in the brain. This means more routes for higher order cognitive functioning. The optimal conditions for synaptic growth would include multiple complex connective challenges where, in learning, we are actively engaged in multi-sensory immersion experiences.

MI theory, according to Gardner, is an endorsement of three key propositions:

- We are not all the same.

- We do not all have the same kinds of minds.

- Education works most effectively if these differences are taken into account rather than denied or ignored.

He suggests that the challenge of the next millennium is whether we can make these differences central to teaching and learning or whether we will instead continue to treat everyone in a uniform way. Gardner proposes "individually configured education" - an education that takes individual differences seriously and crafts practices that serve different kinds of minds equally well. And recognising the fact that we are all unique is clearly central to this process.

References

Berman, M. (2002). *A Multiple Intelligences Road to an ELT Classroom*. Carmarthen: Crown House Publishing.

Berman, M. & D. Brown (2000). *The Power of Metaphor - Story Telling & Guided Journeys for Teachers, Trainers and Therapists*. Carmarthen: Crown House Publishing.

Berman, M. (2010). *In a Faraway Land*. Ropley, Hampshire: O-Books.

Christison, M. A. (2005). *Multiple Intelligences and Language Learning. A Guidebook of Theory, Activities, Inventories, and Resources*. San Fransisco: Alta Books.

Gardner, H. (1983). *Frames of Mind. The Theory of Multiple Intelligences*. New York: Basic Books.

Gardner, H. (1993). *Multiple Intelligences. The Theory in Practice*. New York: Basic Books.

Gardner, H. (1999). *Intelligence Reframed. Multiple Intelligences for the 21st Century*. New York: Basic Books.

Gardner, H. (2006). *Multiple Intelligences: New Horizons*. New York: Basic Books.

Littlemore, J. (2001). "Metaphoric intelligence and foreign language learning." Humanising Language Teaching 3:2.

Zohar, D. & I. Marshall (2000). *SQ - The Ultimate Intelligence*. London: Bloomsbury.

13

Using Jokes, Urban Myths and
Personal Anecdotes in the ELT Classroom

A man goes into a doctor's surgery. The doctor says, "Oh, Mr. Jones! We have the results of your test. Do you want the bad news first or the very bad news?" The man shrugs and says, "Well I guess I'll have the bad news first." "Well the bad news is, you have 24 hours to live," the doctor replies. The man is distraught, "24 hours to live? That's horrible! What could be worse than that? What's the VERY bad news?" The doctor folds his hands and sighs, "The very bad news is...I've been trying to contact you to tell you since yesterday."

When you repeat a joke you have heard, you are in effect telling a story. It is something we do all the time without even realizing it, and telling stories is one of the basic ways that humans communicate with each other.

However, why tell jokes, urban myths or personal anecdotes in the classroom? First of all because, as they entertain and hold people's attention, and if we cannot hold the learners' attention then there is really nothing that we can achieve. Secondly, as they are a means of creating a rapport with people, and without such a rapport again little of value is possible. Last but not least, through such storytelling indirect learning can take place, which is believed to be the most powerful sort of all – when we learn without even realising we are doing so. Here's an example of a joke that could be used with Business English students:

A man needs a job and decides to apply at the zoo. As it happened, their star attraction, a gorilla, had passed away the night before and they had carefully preserved his hide. They tell this man that they'll pay him well if he would dress up in the gorilla's skin and pretend to be the gorilla so people will keep coming to the zoo. Well, the man has his doubts, but Hey! He needs the money, so he puts on the skin and goes out into the cage. The people all cheer to see him. He plays up to the audience and they just eat it up. This isn't so bad, he thinks, and he starts really putting on a show, jumping around, beating his chest and roaring, swinging around. During one acrobatic attempt, though, he loses his balance and crashes through some safety netting, landing square in the middle of the lion cage! As he lies there stunned, the lion roars. He's terrified and starts screaming, "Help, Help, Help!" The lion races over to him, places his paws on his chest and hisses, "Shut up or we'll BOTH lose our jobs!"

Now, working in small groups, discuss the following questions. Then choose a spokesperson to report back to the rest of the class with your findings:

a. Have you ever lied, cheated or done something else unethical in order to get a job, and do you think such an approach can ever be justified? If so, in what circumstances?

b. Have you ever been discriminated against when applying for a job? Tell me about it.

c. What advice would you give to help a school leaver successfully negotiate his or her first job interview?

d. "Anybody can find a job if they are determined enough, regardless of the economic situation." – What do you think of this statement?

The Dogs Hold an Election

Pre-Listening: Some people say that all politicians are the same and it doesn't matter very much who you vote for because nothing ever changes. Here's an American Indian story which suggests an alternative way of choosing a suitable candidate!

While-listening: While you're listening to the story, see if you can find the answers to the following questions:

a. Why was the bulldog an unsuitable candidate?
b. Why was the greyhound an unsuitable candidate?
c. What kind of dog suggested a solution to the problem?
d. What was the solution and what do you think of it?

Once a long time ago, the dogs were trying to elect a president. So one of them got up in the big dog convention and said: "I nominate the bulldog for president. He's strong. He can fight."

"But he can't run," said another dog. "What good is a fighter who can't run? He won't catch anybody."

Then another dog got up and said: "I nominate the greyhound, because he can definitely run."

But the other dogs objected: "He can run all right but he can't fight. When he catches up with somebody, what happens then? He gets beaten up, that's what! So all he's good for is running away."

Then an ugly little mongrel jumped up and said: "I nominate that dog for president who smells good underneath his tail."

And immediately an equally ugly mongrel jumped up and yelled: "I second the motion." At once all the dogs started sniffing underneath each other's tails. A big chorus went up:

"Phew, he doesn't smell good under his tail."

"No, neither does this one."

"He's certainly no presidential prospect!" "No, he's no good, either."

"This one certainly isn't the people's choice."

"Wow, this isn't my candidate!"

When you go out for a walk, just watch the dogs. They're still sniffing underneath each other's tails. They're still looking for a good leader, and they still haven't found him.

Post-listening: If it were your responsibility to help elect a President at a political Party Convention, what qualities would you look for in the candidates under consideration, and why? Ask the learners, working in groups, to produce a list of qualities they consider to be important for such a post. Then invite a spokesperson for each group to present the list they have produced to the whole class, so the lists can be compared and contrasted.

Alternatively, why would or wouldn't you be a suitable candidate to be the next President or Prime Minister of your country? Produce a couple of sentences about yourself in answer to this question, which you can then share with the person sitting next to you.

 "I have been to Hell and back, and let me tell you, it was wonderful." – Louise Bourgeois.

If there is a heaven and a hell, what do you imagine these places are like, and how do you suppose people spend their time in these places? Here is a possible answer:

Heaven and Hell

One day while walking down the street a highly successful HR Manager was tragically hit by a bus and she died. Her soul arrived up in heaven where she was met at the Pearly Gates by St. Peter himself.

"Welcome to Heaven," said St. Peter. "Before you get settled in though, it seems we have a problem. You see, strangely enough, we've never once had a Human Resources Manager make it this far and we're not really sure what to do with you."

"No problem, just let me in," said the woman. "Well, I'd like to," replied St. Peter, "but I have higher orders. What we're going to do is let you have a day in Hell and a day in Heaven and then you can choose whichever one you want to spend an eternity in."

"Actually, I think I've made up my mind, I prefer to stay in Heaven," said the woman.

"Sorry, but we have rules and we have to follow them." And with that St. Peter put the executive in a lift and it went down-down-down to hell. The doors opened and she found herself stepping out onto the putting green of a beautiful golf course. In the distance was a country club and standing in front of her were all her friends - fellow executives that she had worked with and they were all dressed in evening gowns and cheering for her. They ran up and kissed her on both cheeks and they talked about old times. They played an excellent round of golf and at night went to the country club where she enjoyed an excellent steak and lobster dinner. She met the Devil who was actually quite a nice bloke and she had a great time telling jokes and dancing. She was having such a good time that before she knew it, it was time to leave. Everybody shook her hand and waved good-bye as she got into the lift. The lift went up-up-up and opened back up at the Pearly Gates and she found St. Peter waiting for her.

"Now it's time to spend a day in heaven," he said. So she spent the next 24 hours lounging around on clouds and playing the harp and singing. She had a great time and before she knew it her 24 hours were up and St. Peter came and got her. "So, you've spent a day in hell and you've spent a day in heaven. Now you must choose your eternity," he said. The woman paused for a second and then replied, "Well, I never thought I'd say this, I mean, Heaven has been really great and all, but I think I had a better time in Hell." So St. Peter escorted her to the lift and again she went down-down-down back to Hell.

When the doors of the elevator opened she found herself standing in a desolate wasteland covered in rubbish and filth. She saw her friends were dressed in rags and were picking up the rubbish and putting it in sacks. The Devil came up to her and put his arm around her.

"I don't understand," stammered the woman, "yesterday I was here and there was a golf course and a country club and we ate lobster and we danced and had a great time. Now all there is, is a wasteland of rubbish and all my friends look miserable."

The Devil looked at her and smiled. "Yesterday we were recruiting you, today you're staff..."

*

Without looking back at the text, place all the parts of the joke in the correct order:

a. "Actually, I think I've made up my mind, I prefer to stay in Heaven,"said the woman.

b. "I don't understand," stammered the woman, "yesterday I was here and there was a golf course and a country club and we ate lobster and we danced and had a great time. Now all there is, is a wasteland of rubbish and all my friends look miserable."

c. "No problem, just let me in," said the woman. "Well, I'd like to," replied St. Peter, "but I have higher orders. What we're going to do is let you have a day in Hell and a day in Heaven and then you can choose whichever one you want to spend an eternity in."

d. "Now it's time to spend a day in heaven," he said. So she spent the next 24 hours lounging around on clouds and playing the harp and singing. She had a great time and before she knew it her 24 hours were up and St. Peter came and got her. "So, you've spent a day in hell and you've spent a day in heaven. Now you must choose your eternity," he said. The woman paused for a second and then replied, "Well, I never thought I'd say this, I mean, Heaven has been really great and all, but I think I had a better time in Hell." So St. Peter escorted her to the lift and again she went down-down-down back to Hell.

e. One day while walking down the street a highly successful HR Manager was tragically hit by a bus and she died. Her soul arrived up in heaven where she was met at the Pearly Gates by St. Peter himself.

f. "Sorry, but we have rules and we have to follow them." And with that St. Peter put the executive in a lift and it went down-down-down to hell. The doors opened and she found herself stepping out onto the putting green of a beautiful golf course. In the distance was a country club and standing in front of her were all her friends - fellow executives that she had worked with and they were all dressed in evening gowns and cheering for her. They ran up and kissed her on both cheeks and they talked about old times. They played an excellent round of golf and at night went to the country club where she enjoyed an excellent steak and lobster dinner. She met the Devil who was actually quite a nice bloke and she had a great time telling jokes and dancing. She was having such a good time that before she knew it, it was time to leave. Everybody shook her hand and waved good-bye as she got into the lift. The lift went up-up-up and opened back up at the Pearly Gates and she found St. Peter waiting for her.

g. The Devil looked at her and smiled. "Yesterday we were recruiting you, today you're staff..."

h. "Welcome to Heaven," said St. Peter. "Before you get settled in though, it seems we have a problem. You see, strangely enough, we've never once had a Human Resources Manager make it this far and we're not really sure what to do with you."

i. When the doors of the lift opened she found herself standing in a desolate wasteland covered in rubbish and filth. She saw her friends were dressed in rags and were picking up the rubbish and putting it in sacks. The Devil came up to her and put his arm around her.

1 ___ 2 ___ 3 ___ 4 ___ 5 ___ 6 ___ 7 ___ 8 ___ 9 ___

ANSWERS: 1e / 2h / 3c /4a / 5f / 6d /7i / 8b / 9g

And here are some unintended jokes. These are genuine answers (from 16 year olds) to questions set in last year's (2009) GCSE examination in Swindon, Wiltshire (U.K.), and were submitted by Cécile Marit from Belgium to the online publication www. hltmag.co.uk See if you can work out what makes them funny:

Q. Name the four seasons.
A. Salt, pepper, mustard and vinegar.

Q. Explain one of the processes by which water can be made safe to drink.
A. Flirtation makes water safe to drink because it removes large pollutants like grit, sand, dead sheep and canoeists.

Q. What guarantees may a mortgage company insist on?
A. If you are buying a house they will insist that you are well endowed.

Q. In a democratic society, how important are elections?
A. Very important. Sex can only happen when a male gets an election.

Q. What happens to your body as you age?
A. When you get old, so do your bowels and you get intercontinental.

Q. What happens to a boy when he reaches puberty?
A. He says goodbye to his boyhood and looks forward to his adultery.

Q. What is artificial insemination?
A. When the farmer does it to the bull instead of the cow.

Q. How can you delay milk turning sour?
A. Keep it in the cow.

Q. What is the most common form of birth control?
A. Most people prevent contraception by wearing a condominium.

Q. Give the meaning of the term 'Caesarean section'.
A. The caesarean section is a district in Rome

Q. What is a terminal illness?
A. When you are sick at the airport.

Q. What does the word 'benign' mean?
A. Benign is what you will be after you be eight.

Q. What is a turbine?
A. Something an Arab or Shriek wears on his head.

An urban myth, also known as an urban legend, is a widely circulated story, often believed to be true by the teller, but usually distorted, exaggerated or fabricated for sensational effect, and often having elements of humour or horror. Here are some examples adapted for classroom use:

The first example is entitled *The Autopsy*. You'll need to listen carefully because I'm going to stop before the final sentence and ask you to tell me what you think it is:

The Autopsy

A medical student was trying hard to qualify as a doctor in

Scotland, and was finding the first part of the course heavy going. As the examination weeks drew to a close, her social life had become non-existent and she was nearing exhaustion. Worse still, the final test was the dreaded anatomy practical.

The examining consultant ushered the students into the autopsy theatre with a sympathetic smile and the instructions for the dissection were carefully read out as the class gathered nervously around the shrouded body on the slab.

"We're lucky today", the pathologist announced. "We've got a nice fresh young road victim from down south to dissect. We normally get stuck cutting up some old corpse with no muscle tone, degenerated organs and far from agreeable appearance, not to mention the smell. I think you lot will be pleasantly surprised". At this point the sheet was removed and one of the women students fainted.

"Don't worry, my dear, cadavers often make people go weak at the knees", oozed the pathologist in a patronising fashion as the girl came round a few minutes later. "This often happens when you see a body for the first time".

"That wasn't the problem", she assured him when she came round. "I've seen dead bodies many times before. The problem was _____"

ANSWER: ... that it was the body of my fiancé – he was driving up to Scotland to meet me here!"

***

For the next example, *It's a Dog's Life*, listen to the story, and then decide what the most suitable moral would be. If you do not think any of the listed suggestions are appropriate, then find one of your own.

a. Once bitten, twice shy.
b. Blood is thicker than water.
c. Don't bite the hand that feeds you.
d. When the cat's away, the mice will play.
e. You can't teach an old dog new tricks.

A man comes home from the pub one night, where he spent the evening with his friends, and notices his old faithful Doberman sprawled out on the living room floor, choking on something. At this point, his wife storms in to the room and tells her husband that the dog just started choking, and she didn't know what he'd got hold of. The man then noticed a trail of blood. The trail led up the stairs, into the bedroom, and under the bed where he found the man his wife had been having an affair with for months—two of his fingers were missing.

The Hitchhiker can be introduced by asking the learners what their favourite form of transport is, and why, and this can be followed by inviting them to tell each other about any interesting experiences or encounters they have had while travelling:

A man was driving down a dark country road on his way home from work. He was driving along and he saw a young girl, about 17 or 18 years old, standing at the side of the road. He pulled over and picked her up. He asked her what she was doing out there all alone, and she said she needed to get home very quickly before her parents got upset. So the man took her home, watched her go inside and then he left.

As he drove off he noticed that she had left her sweater in his car, so he decided he would bring it back to her tomorrow. He drove home and went to bed. The next morning after breakfast, he went to return the sweater. When he arrived, he knocked on the door and an old woman answered the door. He held out the sweater and told the lady that the girl had left it in his car the night before. All of a sudden the lady started crying. After she had calmed down a bit, she then said, "There's no way she could have left that in your car, she's been dead for the last 40 years!"

Apparently, the young lady was on her way home from a high school dance when her boyfriend and her got in to a car accident and died instantly. The ghost of the young lady hangs around, getting men of all ages to pick her up and take her home - always leaving something behind.

***

For my final example, *The Narrow Escape*, listen to the story to discover why the girl returned to her room to find it surrounded by police:

There was a girl who went back to the room in a student hostel she shared with a friend, after an evening out, to retrieve her books before heading over to her boyfriends' place to spend the night. She entered the room, but knowing her roommate would be sleeping, she didn't turn on the light.

She stumbled around the room in the dark for several minutes, gathering what she would need before finally leaving. The next afternoon, she came back to her room to find the place surrounded by police.

When asked if she lived there, she replied with a yes. They took her into the room, and there, written on the wall in blood, were the words "Aren't you glad you didn't turn on the light?"

Notes for teachers

Pre-listening: Listen to the story to find out why the girl returned to her room to find it surrounded by police.

Post-listening: Have you ever had a narrow escape from what could have been a disaster, or do you know anybody who has? Tell the person sitting next to you about it.

An alternative way of dealing with this urban myth in class, would be to stop after "and there, written on the wall in blood, were the words ...", and ask the learners to predict the ending.

***

As for the telling of anecdotes, like the example that follows, by sharing such personal information you stop being anonymous, make yourself more approachable, and the learners will then feel less inhibited about doing the same and sharing with you and each other:

The Ghost of the Hardworking Tailor

Anyone who knows me will also know how much I enjoy telling stories, most of which, I have to confess, are entirely invented This tale, however, is one of the few true ones I tell, even though you are unlikely to believe it is once you hear what I have to relate.

When I was a child we lived in a semi-detached house in a suburb of London that had been built on a Second World War bomb site. My bedroom was on the first floor, sharing a common wall with our neighbours' bedroom, and the headboard of my bed backed on to that wall.

Every night, at precisely two o' clock in the morning I was woken up by the sound of a machine – it sounded like an old-fashioned sewing machine, the kind you have to pedal. Not only did I hear it, but also my parents and sister, and anyone else who happened to come to stay with us. And as it stopped me from sleeping, I asked my parents to go next door to find out from the neighbours what they were doing at that time of night, and whether they could stop whatever it was. To their surprise, they learnt that the neighbours had been planning to ask us exactly the same question as they had been kept awake by the same sound too.

That was when we decided to do some research and my mother visited the local library to see what she could find out. What she learnt was that before the War, a tailor had lived in the house that had stood where ours now was, and had been working on his machine when a bomb fell and killed him.

Now this was not really a problem as we got used to the sound, just as you can get used to anything that happens on a daily basis. And when it started, as it invariably would do, at 2.00 am religiously twenty four seven, the reaction would be *nothing to worry about - it's just the tailor at it again*. However, one night something happened that I'll never forget and changed my life forever.

I woke up in the middle of the night cold and shivering, and noticed the bottom of the mattress, where my feet were, seemed to be lower than the rest of the bed and I could feel the weight of someone sitting there. I didn't see anyone, just felt the weight, and was so terrified that I was frozen with fear. I tried to scream but nothing would come out. This lasted for I don't know how long, I suppose just a matter of minutes, before the mattress sprang back to its original position, and everything returned to normal again.

This only ever happened once, but the nightly sound of the machine starting up could be heard for as long as we lived in the house, heard by me, my family, and by everyone else who came to stay with us. I can't explain it, and probably never will be able to, but all I know is that it definitely happened – of that I'm certain.

The Ghost of the Hardworking Tailor: Worksheet (i)

Without looking back at the text, place all the parts of the story in the correct order:

a. And as it stopped me from sleeping, I asked my parents to go next door to find out from the neighbours what they were doing at that time of night, and whether they could stop whatever it was.

b. Anyone who knows me will also know how much I enjoy telling stories, most of which, I have to confess, are entirely invented This tale, however, is one of the few true ones I tell, even though you are unlikely to believe it is once you hear what I have to relate.

c. Every night, at precisely two o' clock in the morning I was woken up by the sound of a machine – it sounded like an old-fashioned sewing machine, the kind you have to pedal. Not only did I hear it, but also my parents and sister, and anyone else who happened to come to stay with us.

d. I didn't see anyone, just felt the weight, and was so terrified that I was frozen with fear. I tried to scream but nothing would come out. This lasted for I don't know how long, I suppose just a matter of minutes, before the mattress sprang back to its original position, and everything returned to normal again.

e. I woke up in the middle of the night cold and shivering, and noticed the bottom of the mattress, where my feet were, seemed to be lower than the rest of the bed and I could feel the weight of someone sitting there.

f. Now this was not really a problem as we got used to the sound, just as you can get used to anything that happens on a daily basis. And when it started, as it invariably would do, at 2.00 am religiously twenty four seven, the reaction would be *nothing to worry about - it's just the tailor at it again.* However, one night something happened that I'll never forget and changed my life forever.

g. That was when we decided to do some research and my mother visited the local library to see what she could find out. What she learnt was that before the War, a tailor had lived in the house that had stood where ours now was, and had been working on his machine when a bomb fell and killed him.

h. This only ever happened once, but the nightly sound of the machine starting up could be heard for as long as we lived in the house, heard by me, my family, and by everyone else who came to stay with us. I can't explain it, and probably never will be able to, but all I know is that it definitely happened – of that I'm certain.

i. To their surprise, they learnt that the neighbours had been planning to ask us exactly the same question as they had been kept awake by the same sound too.

j. When I was a child we lived in a semi-detached house in a suburb of London that had been built on a Second World War bomb site. My bedroom was on the first floor, sharing a common wall with our neighbours' bedroom, and the headboard of my bed backed on to that wall.

1 ___ 2 ___ 3 ___ 4 ___ 5 ___ 6 ___ 7 ___ 8 ___ 9 ___ 10 ___

The Ghost of the Hardworking Tailor: Worksheet (ii)

Gerund or Infinitive? Find someone who:

Enjoys getting up early in the morning (Find out why, and at what time)

Has considered changing their job (Find out what they'd like to do instead)

Can imagine becoming famous one day (Find out in what field)

Has attempted to break a world record (Find out what sort of record)

Has decided to stay in _____ permanently (Find out why)

Hopes to take an exam in English (Find out which one, and why)

Is planning to go somewhere really special on holiday this year (Find out where)

Keeps making the same mistake in their spoken English (Find out which mistake)

Has resolved to get married this year, or to have children (Find out why)

Doesn't mind doing lots of homework or working overtime

Has risked losing their job or the person they love by coming to _____

Will agree to take you for a drink after class this evening

Resents having to study English or having to work as a _____ (Find out why)

Will offer to lend you money or to put you up in their flat or to marry you

14

English Through the Writing on Your Forehead

Astrology, Palmistry, Claivoyance, and the I-Ching have all been used to foretell the future. Have you ever been to a fortune-teller? Why or why not? What other methods of telling the future are you familiar with? Do you practise any yourself? Invite the learners to discuss these questions in pairs or small groups, and then to report back with their findings. Use this activity as a lead-in to the story and guided visualisation that follow:

Armenians even today believe that there is writing on a person's forhead which tells his or her future and that this future is pre-determined. The Writer, or Grog, who is responsible for recording this is believed by many to be the good angel who sits on the right shoulder of each of us, urging us to do good things and keeping accurate records of such doings. The bad angel, on the other hand, sits on the left shoulder and encourages us to do wrong. This writer, Tir, was believed to be the scribe of the supreme god, Aramazd (see Hoogasian-Villa, 1966, p.323).

The story that follows was taken from 100 Armenian Tales and their Folkloristic Relevance, collected and edited by Susie Hoogasian-Villa and published by Wayne State University Press, Detroit, 1966.

Foretelling the Future

The wife of a farmer was taking care of the sheep in the fields when she gave birth to a child. A shepherd nearby saw an angel descend from heaven and write something on the baby's forehead. But since the shepherd could not see what was written, he asked the angel, "What did you do to that child?"

"I wrote his future on his forehead," the angel said.

"Why? Is he such an unusual child?"

"All human beings have their future written on their foreheads when they are born," the angel said, preparing to leave. "This child will fall from a tree and die at the age of seven."

The shepherd was very much interested: "I'll ask that woman's name, and after seven years, I will return to see if the angel's prediction comes true." And this he did.

After seven years he decided to find the woman and see how the child was. He found her house but saw that there was a large crowd gathered around it. "What has happened?" he asked a neighbor.

"The little boy who live here fell from a tree and died, and the parents want to kill the other boy who was playing with him. They say that because their son died, his playmate must die, too. Of course the playmate's parents won't permit this, and so the two families are quarreling."

"Oh, oh! The angel was right," the man said to himself, "but one death is enough. I must try to stop the second." He pushed through the crowd, went inside the house and asked the family about the trouble.

The first woman said, "My son was playing in the tree with this woman's son, and my boy fell off the tree and died. This woman's son should die, too."

"If your son fell off, why should my son die?" the second woman asked.

"Listen to me for a minute," the shepherd said. "Do you remember me?" he asked the first woman. "I am the shepherd you saw on the day your son was born in the fields. That same day, at the same time your son was born, an angel came down from heaven and wrote on his forehead. I asked the angel what he had written, and I was told that the little boy would fall from a tree at the age of seven and die. Now it has happened, and no one is to blame. Come, spare this little boy's life."

The first woman, seeing the truth of the argument, stopped asking for the life of the little boy. "What God has determined, we cannot prevent," she said.

Choose three of the following questions to ask the person sitting next to you. Then report back what you found out to the rest of the class:

a. What feelings did you have during the telling of the story?
b. Have you ever been in a similar situation to any of the characters in the tale?
c. Did any of the characters remind you of people you know?
d. What do you think the "message" of the story is?
e. Did it remind you of any other stories you know?
f. Which was the most moving or memorable bit of the story for you?
g. Which bit of the story sent you off to sleep?

Tir (Apollo) - the god of literature, science and art, also an interpreter of dreams.

What follows is a guided visualisation based on the story presented above. If you are working on your own, it is suggested that you record the script, perhaps with some appropriate background music. You can then lie somewhere comfortable, where you will not be disturbed, and play the recording back to yourself as you go through the process described.

The Mirror that Shows Your Future

SCRIPT FOR THE GUIDE: (To be read in a gentle trance-inducing voice). Make yourself comfortable and close your eyes. Take a few deep breaths to help you relax. Feel the tension disappear stage by stage from the top of your head to the tips of your toes. Let your surroundings fade away as you gradually sink backwards through time and actuality and pass through the gateway of this reality into the dreamtime. (When the participants are fully relaxed, begin the next stage).

Today's a very special day for you because you're being given an opportunity to see your future and, more importantly, to make changes now to ensure you have the best possible chance of turning it into what you want it to be.

Ahead of you what appears to be some kind of temple. Up three stone steps you make your way to an arched oak-panelled doorway. The doors are wide open for you, and within a deep blue carpet runs down the central aisle. At the end of it an indistinct figure swaying a censer perfumed with frankincense to and fro, enveloped by smoke. Breathe it in and feel centred. The smoke obscures your vision, but only

temporarily, for as it clears the figure becomes clear to you –
Tir the scribe and the keeper of the records. He stands by a
full-length mirror. Notice both its distinct frame and shape. It
shape seems to be that of a human body, your body in fact.

Tir motions to you to approach and join him, where he
invites you to stand in front of the mirror and to look into it,
in particular to see what is written on your forehead. And you
have a minute of clock time, equal to all the time you need for
this ...

You're probably now wondering what you can do to
change what you see. What you can do is work towards
making a better future for yourself and those you interact
with by learning from the mistakes you've made and by
making sure you don't repeat them again. The time has come
now for Tir to speak. And you have a minute of clock time,
equal to all the time you need, to hear what advice he has to
give you on this subject ...

You can make those changes that you really wish to make,
for your unconscious mind is listening and will receive and
act upon the messages it hears. And you will find, as this is
happening, that you become much happier, within yourself -
delighted with who you are, what you have and everything
you can offer. What matters now, is that you take what you
have learnt back with you and that you hold on to it. The time
has come to give thanks for what you have received and to
take your leave, to make your way back, down the carpeted
central aisle of the temple, through the arched wooden doors,
down the three steps and back to the place where you started
from, where your new life awaits you.

Take a deep breath, let it all out slowly, open your eyes,
and smile at the first person you see. Stretch your arms,
stretch your legs, stamp your feet on the ground, and make
sure you're really back, back in (name of the location), back
where you started from. Welcome home!

Now take a few minutes in silence to make some notes on the experiences you had on your journeys, which you can then share with the rest of the group.

Or

Now take a few minutes in silence to make some notes on the experiences you had on your journeys, which you can then make a note of in your dream journal.

Or

And now you might like to turn to the person sitting next to you and share some of the experiences you had on your journeys.

***

As well as finding out about the future from the writing on your forehead, it is possible to do so from your handwriting too – through the study of graphology. So, as a follow-up activity, you can invite the learners to each copy the following note on to a piece of blank, preferably unlined, paper:

Dear Michael

This is just a short note to thank you for giving me the opportunity to change my future for the better in your workshop today. I found the session extremely ....

Yours sincerely

(Signature)

Next ask the students to exchange their notes with a partner, present them with details of what they should look for in the writing (see the points below), and give them time to analyse the samples they have. Once this stage is completed, they return the samples to their owners and present them with their findings.

The accuracy of these findings can then be discussed by the learners in pairs, small groups, or by the class as a whole, to bring the lesson to a close.

What to look for:

- The relative size of the upper (religious/spiritual), middle (work/domestic) and lower (emotional/sexual) zones of the letters indicates what your priorities are at this point in time
- The upper and lower zones crossing each other – unrealistic expectations
- Unnecessarily wide margins surrounding the letter: on the left – past problems the writer would like to escape from , on the right – future uncertainty / above – existential problems / below – emotional uncertainties or fears
- The pressure of the pen on the page: heavy – under a lot of pressure / light – full of energy or artistic/sensitive
- The style – angular (a quick temper) or cursive (a gentle nature)
- The relative size of the signature compared with the writing in the letter (how honest you are). Ideally they should be the same size.
- The colour of the ink used: black – professional / blue - home-loving / red - attention-seeking / green - aggressive
- The dot above the letter i: to the right – a quick thinker / to the left – a time-waster / directly above – a dependable person
- The roundness and openness of the vowels – how honest or talkative you are
- Capital letters within words for no apparent reason – a sign of eccentricity

***

WHO AM I? WHERE AM I? or WHAT'S MY PROBLEM? For another way of telling someone their future from their foreheads, stick pre-prepared prompt cards on the foreheads of everyone in your class. Then ask them to pair up and try to guess who they are, where they are, or what their problems are, by questioning their partners. However, they can only ask YES or NO questions, a maximum of 20, in order to find the answers they are looking for.

15

How to Cater for
Intrapersonal Intelligence

Howard Gardner's Multiple Intelligences Theory accounts for why certain learners object to working in pairs despite the fact that it clearly increases STT in class – Student Talking Time. Gardner defines Intrapersonal intelligence as the capacity to understand oneself – including one's own desires, fears, and capacities – and to use such information effectively in regulating one's own life. Learners with high Intrapersonal Intelligence prefer having an opportunity to look within first before discussing their thoughts with others and failure to cater for this fact in class can only lead to resentment. The following activity is designed with this aim in mind as it gives learners time to work independently before group work takes place:

20 ways to make the world a better place

Have a look at this list and decide which suggestions you would be willing to take up. Then add five suggestions of your own. Now get into groups to share your ideas:

1. Wear bright clothes once a week. It will cheer everyone up.
2. Telephone or write to someone you haven't seen for five years.
3. Take a plant into your office or take a packet of biscuits and buy everyone a cup of tea.
4. Turn off your TV and do something less boring instead.
5. Keep a bowl of fruit on your desk at work.

6. Pray. Not necessarily to God, just say a short prayer offering thanks at the end of each day.
7. Risk ridicule – smile at strangers, talk to shop assistants.
8. If you see someone lost, show them the way.
9. Don't push in crowds.
10. Stop yourself saying "I".
11. Take action on things you think are wrong or offensive.
12. If you have any clothes you haven't worn for a year, give them away – to friends, relatives or charity shops.
13. Plant a tree. Put one in your garden or a local communal space.
14. Listen to children as you listen to adults – give them as many rights as you give yourself.
15. Take responsibility for your problems and don't blame others for the situations you find yourself in.
16. ....
17. ....
18. ....
19. ....
20. ....

Intrapersonal intelligence indicates the ability to look within for causes and to find solutions to problems and is perhaps the most neglected Intelligence type for teaching purposes. Circle-time provides an ideal way of catering for it in class – a group working together in a safe situation where there are agreed rules, working on personal contributions, affirmations, active and reflective listening and celebrations. Essay titles such as Mistakes I Won't Repeat, My Life in the Future, How I'd be different if I'd grown up in a different culture, How a Martian might describe me etc can also help to facilitate looking within. Another technique that can prove to be effective is pole-bridging - having students describe aloud what they are doing as they do it. Encourage them to reflect on what has been done and to speculate on what is to come.

Creative writing, especially poetry, involves looking within and appeals to the intrapersonal intelligence type. The following poem by Emily Dickinson can be used for work on conditionals. The students can be invited to write their own version of the poem, starting with the words "If I can ..." and ending with "... I shall not live in vain."

If I can stop one heart from breaking
I shall not live in vain;
If I can ease one life the aching
Or cool one pain;
Or help one fainting robin
Unto his nest again,
I shall not live in vain

Something learnt from an experience that includes deeper and wider purposes will be more readily and more fully available for future performance than an item from an experience that has included only shallower, smaller-scale purposes. The following activity that springs from a poem can be used to reinforce the teaching point that the zero article is employed when talking about a subject in general. Moreover, it is being dealt with indirectly – the conscious attention of the learner is being deflected from the goal – another reason why the information is more likely to be retained in the long term memory:

Time is
Too slow for those who wait
Too long for those who grieve
Too short for those who rejoice
But for those who love
Time is eternity

Now write a parallel poem, using the same format, on the subject of *Money* or *Work*:

> ... is ...
> Too ... for those who ...
> Too ... for those who ...
> Too ... for those who ...
> But for those who ...
> ... is ...

The activity can be adapted to fit into a topic-based approach. Other subjects to write parallel poems about could include *Love, Food, Sleep, Sunshine* and *Rain*.

***

Pictures can be used to focus on, and cater for, the Intrapersonal Intelligence type in class too, in order to facilitate creative writing:

The Gift

What would you give the person you love if you could? Write a poem to him / her:

If I could I'd _____ with _____
And I'd _____
Then I'd _____ like _____
That it's all for you and nobody else – If.

And here is a sample poem. How does it compare with yours?

If I could I'd shower you with kisses like raindrops
I'd lay you on a bed of cherry blossom
With a pillow of petals for your head
I'd crown you with a circle of sunbeams
And hang daisy chains around your neck
Then I'd whisper like the wind through the leaves
That it's all for you and nobody else – If.

What was the last present you actually gave to or received from someone you love? Or what is the present you'd most like to be given, and why? Tell the person sitting next to you about it.

***

Limericks can also be made use of to cater for intrapersonal learners. You can display a limerick on an overhead transparency, for example the one about a man from Beijing, and then let the students find out which words on which lines rhyme with which words:

There once was a man from Beijing.
All his life he hoped to be King.
So he put on a crown,
Which quickly fell down.
That small silly man from Beijing.

Next, hand out the templates for creating basic limericks shown below and ask the students to work individually and produce at least two limericks of their own:

Template A

There once was a _____ from _____

All the while s/he hoped _____

So s/he _____

And _____

That _____ from _____.

Template B

I once met a _____ from _____

Every day s/he _____

But whenever s/he _____

The _____

That strange_____ from_____.

***

Two further activities are presented below which can be used to facilitate creative writing. They are not only non-threatening but also good fun and can provide a lead-in to more ambitious projects:

For each letter of the alphabet, write a word that starts with that letter. Then write at least three sentences that use words from your list in sequence. Use as many of the words in combinations as you can, then compare results with the person sitting next to you.

The **d**runk **E**nglish **f**ootball supporters started a fight outside the stadium.
Go **h**ome **i**diots!
Two **u**gly **v**iolinists played a duet.

Write four sentences following the format below:

Who	What	Where
The tourist guide	spat at the tourists	in Westminster Anney
The film star	wore a pink dress	at the Awards Ceremony
The policeman	broke down	and wept in court
The monkey	climbed up a tree	in the jungle

Switch the parts around so each WHO has a new WHAT and WHERE, then compare results with the person sitting next to you.

Interpersonal intelligence is well catered for in most course books, with there being plenty of activities for pair or group work built into them. Activities to cater Intrapersonal intelligence, on the other hand, seem to be few and far between. This could well be due to the fact that our preferences as teachers are very much based on our own particular strengths and weaknesses. In other words, the Intelligence types we best cater for are those which we tend to score highly on. Hopefully, the suggestions and material presented in this Chapter can help to redress the balance.

References

Berman, M. (2002). A *Multiple Intelligences Road to an ELT Classroom*. Carmarthen: Crown House Publishing.

Gardner, H. (1983). *Frames of Mind. The Theory of Multiple Intelligences*, New York: Basic Books.

Gardner, H. (1993). *Multiple Intelligences. The Theory in Practice*. New York: Basic Books.

Gardner, H. (1999). *Intelligence Reframed. Multiple Intelligences for the 21st Century*. New York: Basic Books.

Gardner, H. (2006). *Multiple Intelligences*: New Horizons. New York: Basic Books.

Palmberg, R. (2010) *Basic Multiple Intelligences for EFL Teachers*, Finland: Palmsoft Publications.

16

Using Circles in the ELT Classroom

Weekly Rounds: The idea is for everyone to sit in a circle and to take it in turns to say how they are feeling and what they would like to have more or e are really getting what they want. And if the answer is "no", then the session provides an opportunity to bring about change. After such a feedback session, a programme can be planned for the following week taking everyone's views into account.

The person who is talking holds a talisman or a Talking Stick, which is passed round the circle. Whoever holds the Talking Stick cannot be interrupted. This way everybody gets to talk when it is their turn. People can talk about anything they want, but nothing that is said may be repeated elsewhere. This helps people talk honestly. The Native American Talking Stick reminds us that to speak is a privilege. Words are sacred. They are magical. They can be builders or destroyers and they can bring peace or pain. For many people the tongue is the most intransigent organ of the body, seemingly with a will of its own. To select one's words with care and thoughtfulness is to speak in a sacred manner. The Talking Stick helps us awaken from the stupor of too many words and of good words that have been used in evil ways. It is one of the most important tools of the circler.

Spiral Learning: Instead of linear instruction, where the learning is introduced once, then never again, spiral instructions can help to activate knowledge into meaning. A single topic might be brought up four or five times. This is also known as layered learning. Past learning is part of the learner's pereptual maps. Therefore, the learner needs to integrate into the new learning what they know or it may not be accepted.

Musical Chairs: The following version of the game is an effective way of putting the Total physical Response approach into practice with young learners. If there are sixteen people, then use fifteen chairs, which they walk around in circles. When they hear a word that does not fit into the lexical set being presented, they should sit down on the nearest available chair. Whoever is left standing is out, and the number of chairs is then reduced again by one. The process continues until only one chair is left and the winner is found.

Mind-Mapping: These webbed, thematic, graphic organisers offer colourful peripheral thoughts organised around a key idea, often in the form of a circle, and provide an excellent vehicle for understanding associations of ideas. They were popularised by Tony Buzan, Michael Gelb and Nancy Marglies.

Researchers who have studied the use of graphic organisers have found that they do, indeed, help learners understand and recall information better, but they have to be personalised. The mind maps the learners produce can be used for peer teaching purposes to review the material covered.

Chinese Whispers: Write a sentence on a card in large readable letters, a tongue-twister perhaps, then place it face downwards on your table. Whisper the utterance once only to the person next to you, who then repeats the process with his/her neighbour. Work round the circle until you come to the last person who says the utterance aloud to the group. This can then be compared with the original version on the card.

Name Learning: This works rather like the children's game "I went to market" and can be used as a First Day activity. "My name's Michael and I've got no hair. I'd like you to repeat the information I've just given you, and then add your own name and a sentence about yourself." If necessary, you can provide a skeleton on the board as a model:

Your name's _____ and you _____
My name's _____ and I _____

Singing can also be used with a new class to introduce members to one another. One member begins by singing their name to the group and the group responds by repeating it just as it was sung.

Lazy Eights: This is an activity used on Brain Gym to connect left and right brain and to improve motor co-ordination. The idea is to trace the shape of a figure eight in the air with one arm extended in front of you and the thumb pointing upwards. Try this with both arms independently and then with both your hands clasped together. Brain Gym, also known as Educational Kinesiology, was developed by Paul E. Dennison in the 1970s and involves the use of movement to enhance learning potential. It has been found that by carrying out such activities prior to reading/writing tasks, performance can be greatly improved.

The Describe-in-the-Round Game: Invite the students to sit in a circle and give a picture to one of them. Ask that person to make a simple sentence describing the picture – "There's a woman," for example. The picture is then passed on to the next person, who repeats the sentence and adds to it – "There's a woman and she's sitting on a camel." Continue round the circle, with the learners either adding to the original sentence or adding new ones, until somebody forgets something. Although this is quite challenging at lower levels, the person speaking has the picture and this acts as a prompt.

The Rain Game: This not only caters for Naturalist Intelligence but will also appeal to those who learn from movement and get restless when obliged to keep still.

The class stand in a circle, facing the middle and the "conductor" of the activity. By copying the movements made by the conductor, which are listed below, the effects of a storm can be created to set the scene for a role play or perhaps a story. It takes the form of a "Mexican wave" in that the participants only perform the actions when the conductor turns to face them and the conductor is constantly turning on the spot:

1. Rub hands together (the wind)
2. Snap fingers (the rain)
3. Slap hands on thighs
4. Stomp feet (full-blown storm)

Then the order is reversed as the storm blows past:

1. Slap hands on thighs
2. Snap fingers
3. Rub hands together
4. Silence

There follows an alternative version of the game, suitable for larger classes:

The participants start by tapping two fingers together, the point/index fingers. Then after a few seconds, four fingers together, then six, then eight. Then, back down to six, four, two. With a large group of rain makers, it can sound like a hurricane!

Circle Dancing: The Circle can also be used for dance. Circle dance has grown out of the European traditional folk dance community, thanks to a German dancer, Bernard Wosien, who believed that many traditional dances were being lost to modern culture. He travelled through western and eastern Europe collecting and annotating an enormous repertoire of circle dances, which he speculates were the first form of dance. In order to ensure their preservation, he brought them to the Findhorn Foundation in Scotland, which now serves as the guardian of the repertoire.

The story behind these dances is a living, evolving story, as is the case with any art form based in folk traditions. These dances have the power to transport the participants back to a time characterized by a greater sense of community and an under-standing of our relationship to the natural world – a time when people still lived in villages and great forests still stretched across Europe. Some of the dances are so old that their origins are long since lost. All that is known is that they were preformed among the great standing stones of Gaul or in Armenian mountain villages. These dances give form to our images of that time, which rest in our collective unconscious, and the lyrics that accompany the music provide an opportunity to experience the oral traditions and poetic verse through which culture and history were communicated and preserved. In all of this the dances enable those who take part to experience celebration, a sense of community, grounding, affirmation, and healing – all so badly needed in today's world.

Not to worry if you have two left feet because the dances can be very basic and the main purpose is to get into communication. For example, there is a very simple dance that involves everyone moving their left foot to the left on the first beat and bringing their right foot beside the left on the second beat. As in the case of all ceremony, the most powerful process is often the one you create yourself.

The Circle of Compliments: The teacher's role as a facilitator involves creating a supportive environment in which learners can feel good about themselves and produce their best work, where they feel safe to experiment and take risks. The Circle of Compliments, described below, is designed with this aim in mind. It was adapted from an idea in *Handing Over* by Jane Revell and Susan Norman, published by Saffire Press.

The idea is for everyone, teacher included, to form a circle. Working clockwise or anti-clockwise, take it in turns to tell the person next to you something you like about them. Alternatively, everyone can speak as and when they feel ready to do so. The Circle can be used to help bring a group together or as a closing ceremony at the end of a course. As a lead-in to the activity, you might like to pre-teach the following language:

I really like/love

the way you ...

I'd like to thank you for

What I really appreciate/enjoy is   your sense of humour

I think you've got a really
    good/great   dress sense

You're really good at

making people laugh

You've got a great way of

Full Circle can be used for reviewing vocabulary. Write the words for review with their meaning on the board. Tell half the class their job is to remember all the words and meanings. Meanwhile, give the other students one of the words each and ask them to write a question that will elicit the word, e.g. *towel – what do you use to dry yourself with after a bath?*

The learners then stand in two circles. The inner circle with questions faces the outward, and an equal number of students face inwards on the outer circle. The members of the inner circle ask their questions and the members of the outer circle answer.

Then all the learners on the outside move round one place to answer another question, and so on until all have had the chance to answer all the questions. To make the activity more competitive, students can keep a count of the words they got right and the person with the most words wins the fabulous mystery prize!

Spokes of the Wheel: The learners form the "spokes" of the wheel and the teacher is in the centre. When one of the spokes needs help, they turn to the person closest to the centre in their line. That person has a dictionary, preferably an English-English one. If that person needs help, s/he turns to the teacher, to pronounce a word, for example.

The String Tossing Game: All you need for this activity is a ball of string and for all the participants to sit in a circle. Decide on a topic and explain that everyone will have an opportunity to say something about it. Start by providing a model, and then throw the ball of string to whoever wishes to speak while holding on to one end. When the first speaker has finished, he / she holds on to the end of the string and throws the ball on to the next volunteer. After everyone in the circle has contributed, the string connects them. The fact that we are all connected and influence one another in the classroom can be demonstrated by tugging on the string. This enables people to see the effect they can have on each other and that each member of the group is a unique and important contributor to the process.

Circling your Brain Size: Draw a small circle on the whiteboard indicating your brain size. Then draw a much larger circle, indicating the combined brain size of all the learners in your class. This lead-in can be used to encourage people to share their questions, answers and experiences during your lessons. You are not a guru or a rainmaker and nobody should expect you to be one. Often a member of your class might well have a better answer to a question than you can come up with, especially if you are teaching Business English class where the learners may well know a lot more than you when it comes to their area of expertise, and it is important to remember this so you get things in perspective.

The Affirming Circle: Invite the learners to stand up and form a circle. Give each person a card with one word of the chosen affirmation written on it. Ask them to memorize what is on the card, and then return it to you. The idea is for them to then rearrange themselves into the correct order to produce the complete affirmation. When they think they have found the correct order, they can each take it in turns to go to the board and write their word on it. If there are not enough words to go round, those people without cards can help with the rearranging. Some examples of quotations that could be used for the purpose are presented below:

'Concentrate only on those moments in which you achieved what you desired, and this strength will help you to accomplish what you want.'
- Paolo Coelho

'You have the power in the present moment to change limiting beliefs and consciously plant the seeds for the future of your choosing.'
- Serge Kahili King

'We must be willing to get rid of the life we've planned, so as to have the life that is waiting for us.'
- Joseph Campbell

'It's only when we truly know and understand that we have a limited time on earth ... that we will begin to love every day to the fullest, as if it was the only one we had.'
- Elizabeth Kubler Ross

'A man can live out his entire life without ever finding more than what was already within him as his Beginning Gift, but if he wishes to grow he must become a seeker and seek for himself the other ways.'
- Hyemeyohsts Storm

Finally, why use circles in the classroom? Perhaps the answer lies in the following verses:

The Almond-Tree

As the kernel of an almond is spoilt utterly
If it is plucked from its husk while unripe,
So error in the path of the pilgrim
Spoils the kernel of his soul.
When the knower is divinely illumined,
The kernel ripens, bursts the husk,
And departs, returning no more.
But another retains the husk,
Though shining as a. bright sun,
And makes another circuit.
From water and earth springs up into a tree,
Whose high branches are lifted up to heaven;
Then from the seed of this tree
A hundredfold are brought forth.
Like the growth of a seed into the line of a tree,
From point comes a line, then a circle;
When the circuit of this circle is complete,
Then the last is joined to the first.

Intermingling

You are plurality transformed into Unity,
And Unity passing into plurality;
This mystery is understood when man
Leaves the part and merges in the Whole.

***

The above verses are taken from *The Secret Rose Garden* of Sa'd Ud Din Mahmud Shabistari, rendered from the Persian with an Introduction by Florence Lederer. London: J. Murray [1920], scanned, proofed and formatted at sacred-texts.com, September 2005, by John Bruno Hare, and in the public domain.

Sa'd ud Din Mahmud Shabistari was born in Persia, in Shabistar, near Tabriz, about 1250 CE. His best known work, *The Secret Rose Garden* is a set of verses that uses the rich Sufi allegorical language to explore the path back to God, to what we originated from, the only real journey we ever take.

References

Buzan, T. (2009) *The Mind Map Book: Unlock Your Creativity, Boost Your Memory, Change Your Life*, BBC Active.

Dennison, P. E., & Dennison, G.E. (1992) *Brain Gym (Orange)*, Edu-Kinesthetics Inc.

Revell, J. & Norman, S. (1999) *Handing Over: NLP-based Activities for Language Learning*, Saffire Press.

Watts, J. (2006) *Circle Dancing: Celebrating the Sacred in Dance: Celebrating Sacred Dance*, Green Magic.

17

How to Cater for
Interpersonal Intelligence

Howard Gardner defines Interpersonal intelligence as a person's capacity to understand the intentions, motivations, and desires of other people and, consequently, to work effectively with others.

Games which require teamwork for a successful outcome are an ideal way of catering for the Interpersonal Intelligence type. Examples of suitable activities include the ubiquitous *Balloon Debate* and the *Desert Island Consensus Game*. Questionnaires and mock collaborative exercises which require empathy can also be effective tools.

Collective dialogue-writing is another way of providing an opportunity to cater for interpersonal intelligence. The following set of activities was designed for an advanced level class to improve their mastery of the use of the articles by focusing on fixed expressions with the zero article, with the indefinite article, and with the definite article:

Go through the fixed expressions with the class, column by column, to make sure they are understood. Arrange the students in pairs or groups. Ask them to select five of the expressions and incorporate them into a dialogue. Then invite the students to act out their dialogues for the rest of the class:

Health & Medicine

Zero article	The indefinite article	The definite article
to have flu	to have/catch a cold	to feel under the weather

to have indigestion	to go on a diet	What's the matter?
to lose weight	to have a toothache/ back ache	What seems to be the problem?
to suffer from depression	to ask for a second opinion	to be on the mend
to be in pain	three times a day	to be over the worst
to be in good/ safe hands	to have a temperature	to be on the road to recovery
to be/suffer from shock	to have a headache	to have the hiccups
to be in a coma	to be given a clean bill of health	to be out of the woods
to lose consciousness	to have an upset stomach	to have one foot in the grave
to regain consciousness	to be as fit as a fiddle	to buy drugs/ medicine over the counter
to feel out of sorts		
to be out of danger		
on prescription		

Work

Zero article	The indefinite article	The definite article
to go on strike	£ ... a month/year	To be on the dole
to be out of work	to make a good impression	to be paid by the hour
on business	to make more of an effort	to get the sack
at/off work	to be (stuck) in a rut	to work your fingers to the bone
to do/work overtime	to have a nine to five job	to do the dirty work
to be on/off duty	to have a talent/flair for	the unemployed
to have job security	to have a dead-end job	to reach the top
to give someone notice	to work like a slave	to get the hang of something
to be in charge of	to type ..... words a minute	to rub someone up the wrong way
to have no free time	to make an early start	
to get down to work	to have a good working relationship	

to be computer
literate

to have good
interpersonal
skills

What Do You Love Being can be used for pair work or played as a team game to provide practice in the Present Simple to describe regular activities. Two examples of clues and answers are presented below:

> It's a clean job and the people I entertain keep me warm. I get the chance to see a lot of beautiful people with no clothes on and I don't embarrass them. People find me relaxing. What do I love being?
>   You love being a bath!

> People stroke me and give me milk to drink. They let me sit on their laps. I sleep whenever I like and I don't have to work. What do I love being?
>   You love being a cat!

Now think of something you love being. Write three sentences describing things you do on a regular basis. Exchange the information with the person sitting next to you and see if you can guess who or what they are!

***

Making use of questionnaires

Questionnaires appeal to the Interpersonal Intelligence type as they can involve the learners working in groups together. After pre-teaching new vocabulary, arrange the students in groups. Hand out a copy of the questionnaire to an "interviewer" in each group who reads the questions to the other students and takes on the role of the teacher. Only the interviewer should be able to see the copy and he/she presents the questionnaire to the group as a listening activity. Meanwhile, you can circulate to provide any assistance required. The next stage is for the students to add up their scores and assess the results, which can be examined and discussed by the class as a whole. Although the material is inauthentic in that the questionnaires are contrived, the students have an authentic reason for doing the activity - to find out more about themselves:

What kind of candidate are you at interviews?

1.   Why did you leave your last job?
a. I wasn't learning enough and I was looking for a new challenge
b. I've never had a job
c. At a spiritual level I'm still doing that job and all jobs before it
d. My references caught up with me

2.   How would you rate your team playing skills?
a. I would get the rest of the team to rate them for me
b. I don't usually get picked for teams
c. All humankind are my brothers and sisters and we are all one blood
d. Better than all those other bastards

3.   Who are your referees?
a. The Governor of the Bank of England, the Bishop of York, Prince Charles
b. Kevin, a mate from school

c. The 6th century Welsh Druid Ormenrod and the Cherokee Medicine Man Squatting Bison

d. My judge, probation officer, and psychologist

4. What would you say your weaknesses are?

a. An obsessive drive for perfection and total loyalty to whoever I work for

b. Character and bladder

c. You're projecting your own weaknesses on me. I can help heal you.

d. Do you really think I'm going to tell you? I'm not stupid.

5. What are your interests outside work?

a. Charity work with the homeless and self-improvement courses

b. Playing darts

c. Tapping into the karmic consciousness, out of body experiences, and tree hugging

d. Tattooing the last 10 per cent of my body

6. What kind of company do you want to work for?

a. One that is internally engineered to pivot on the point of its consumer interface

b. Anything really. Indoors would be nice

c. One that vibrates on the same frequency as the cosmos itself

d. The sort that gives you a company car, secretary, pension, bonus, and six weeks' holiday

7. What your greatest personal achievement in life so far?

a. Saving someone's life by donating one of kidneys and then re-engineering the hospital administration

b. Winning a beer drinking competition

c. Understanding that we are all dust, all effort is vanity and all business futility

d. Bench pressing 200lb with one arm

8. What are your computer skills?

a. I can rebuild a client server blindfolded

b. I have high scores in three amusement arcades near where I live

c. Within us we all have all skills. My computer skills are perfect but latent.

d. I can carry a top of the range PC and laser printer from a building in under a minute

9. In your opinion, what is the secret of customer service?

a. Whatever you'd like the answer to be

b. Nobody tells me any secrets

c. Keep no secrets from the customer – that is the real secret

d. Respect. They've got to respect you or they get nothing

10. Finally, do you have any questions for us?

a. Why are you all so talented, charming and good looking?

b. Do you know of any other jobs round here?

c. Does your work enrich you spiritually and enlarge your consciousness?

d. Have I got the job and can I have an advance on my pay?

Check Your Answers

Mostly As: Although you have the perfect interview technique, nobody will employ you because you're just too good to be true. You're a know-all, which is why nobody likes you and why you lost your last job as well.

Mostly Bs: The only reason you attend interviews is because

you would lose your benefit if you didn't. You have the vision, drive and personality of a hubcap. Be careful you don't get offered a job in the accounts department.

Mostly Cs: Your last job interview was probably twenty five years ago. Things have moved on since then, except in marketing, where you probably have a bright future. But be prepared to meet some really weird people.

Mostly Ds: Your forthright opinions, rugged individuality and great sense of humour have you marked down for a job in sales. The double glazing or loan sharking industries will welcome you with open arms.

***

Information gap activities

Information Gap activities can be used for both pair and group work and these can be based on articles, or on pictures. If you are familiar with the Interview papers of the Cambridge FCE and CAE exams, you will know that pictures are used for this purpose. Two different versions of the text/picture are prepared – A and B. Pair the A students with the B students. Then they take it in turns to question each other to find the missing information. The role of the teacher is kept to a minimum, thereby maximizing student involvement. The activity reveals the difficulty many learners have in the formation of questions and can provide an opportunity for remedial work – how the structure of the question changes according to whether the question word is the subject or the object of the sentence. This can be illustrated by using the questions who loves you? and who do you love? Two examples of Information Gap activities designed for Intermediate level learners are presented below:

Everything you always wanted to know about the Sun (Version A)

The Sun is the centre of our solar system. It's the star that the Earth spins around and it provides light and heat. It rises in the east and sets in the west and its rays are the most powerful at midday.

It takes .... for the Earth to get round the Sun. Our calendar compensates by having leap years – an extra day every four years. Before they were introduced in 1752, the calendar had slipped 11 days, so the solstice took place on June 10.

The Sun measures 875,000 miles across. It could contain ....

The Sun is 4,600 million years old and is a quarter of a million times closer to us than the next known star.

An eclipse occurs when...
....

The ozone layer is a layer of air high above the Earth, which prevents harmful ultraviolet light from the sun from reaching the Earth. The hole in the ozone layer, which appeared over Antarctica in the 1980s, has led to...

The midsummer solstice, meaning "the standing still of the sun", traditionally occurs on June 21 but can happen on the 22nd, as it did most recently in 1979, or on the 20th, which it will do in 2012.

The first rays of light on midsummer morning will have taken

.... to travel the 93 million miles from the sun.

The Druids celebrate the summer solstice at Stonehenge. The major axis of Stonehenge was carefully aligned with the midwinter and midsummer sun. There are other alignments too, such as with the rising and setting of the moon, and all these suggest that Stonehenge was originally built for ceremonies to mark the annual calendar and seasons. Stonehenge is just one of hundreds of similar stone megaliths in Britain. And our forbears were not alone – ....also built "archeo-astronomical" structures.

Midsummer is traditionally a favourite time of the year for fairies to appear. According to folklore, if you want to see them you must ....

A sundial is a device which consists of a thin piece of metal fixed to a flat surface marked with numbers, which shows the time by the metal making a dark line on the surface as the sun moves across the sky above it.

"The Sun Also Rises" is the title of a book by......................... ...., "Here Comes The Sun" is the title of a song by the Beatles, and there is also a famous painting by Van Gogh called "Sunflowers" A sunflower is a plant usually having a very tall stem and a single large round flat yellow flower, with many thin narrow petals close together.

Everything you always wanted to know about the Sun (Version B)

The Sun is the centre of our solar system. It's the star that the Earth spins around and it provides light and heat. It rises in the east and sets in the west and its rays are the most powerful at midday

It takes 365 days, five hours and 50 minutes for the Earth to get round the Sun. Our calendar compensates by having leap years – an extra day every four years. Before they were introduced in 1752, ...

The Sun measures 875,000 miles across. It could contain more than a million planets the size of Earth.

The Sun is 4,600 million years old and is ....
....than the next known star.

An eclipse occurs when the sun disappears completely or partly from view while the moon is moving between it and the earth.

The ozone layer is a layer of air high above the Earth, which prevents............................. ....
The hole in the ozone layer, which appeared over Antarctica in the 1980s, has led to an increase in the incidences of skin cancer.

The midsummer solstice, meaning .... ,
traditionally occurs on June 21 but can happen on the 22nd, as it did most recently in 1979, or on the 20th, which it will do in 2012.

The first rays of light on midsummer morning will have taken eight-and-a-half minutes to travel the 93 million miles from the sun.

The Druids celebrate the summer solstice at Stonehenge.   The

major axis of Stonehenge was carefully aligned with
.... There are other alignments
too, such as with the rising and setting of the moon, and all
these suggest that Stonehenge was originally built for
ceremonies to mark the annual calendar and seasons.
Stonehenge is just one of hundreds of similar stone megaliths
in Britain. And our forbears were not alone – Egyptian, Greek,
Mayan and South Pacific civilisations also built "archeo-astronomical" structures.

Midsummer is traditionally a favourite time of the year for
.... According to folklore, if you want to see them
you must rub fern seeds on your eyelids at the stroke of
midnight.

A sundial is a device which consists of a thin piece of metal
fixed to a flat surface marked with numbers, which shows the
time by...

"The Sun Also Rises" is the title of a book by Ernest
Hemingway, "Here Comes The Sun" is the title of a song by
the Beatles, and there is also a famous painting by
.... called "Sunflowers" A sunflower is a
plant usually having a very tall stem and a single large round
flat yellow flower, with many thin narrow petals close
together.

Everything you always wanted to know about Water (Version A)

Water is the common name applied to the liquid state of the
hydrogen-oxygen compound. Pure water is ....
.... However, this colour can only be detected
in layers of considerable depth.

Water is the only substance that occurs at ordinary temperatures in all three states of matter – as a solid, a liquid and a
gas. It covers .... in the form
of swamps, lakes, rivers and oceans. It is also the major
constituent of living matter - from 50 to 90 percent of the
weight of living organisms is water.

The world's five oceans, the main areas of sea, are the Atlantic,
the Pacific, the Indian, the Arctic and the Antarctic. And the
longest river is ....

Hydrology is the science concerned with the distribution of
water on the earth, its physical and chemical reactions with
other naturally occurring substances, and its relation to life on
earth.

Rain is the precipitation of liquid drops of water...................
................., about 10,922 mm per year, occurs at Cherrapunji,
in northeastern India, where moisture-laden air from the Bay
of Bengal is forced to rise over the Khasi Hills of Assam State.
A long period when there is little or no rain is known as a
drought.

Clouds are a condensed form of atmospheric moisture
consisting of small water droplets or tiny ice crystals and
rainfall is dependent on their formation. More than 100
different kinds of clouds are distinguishable and ....
.... has introduced a species of artificial
clouds known as contrails. These are formed from the
condensed water vapour ejected as a part of the engine
exhaust gases. They say that .... to
suggest that even in bad things you can always find
something good.

A spa is a fashionable town where water comes out of the ground and people come to drink or lie in it because they think it will improve their health. Baden Baden in Germany and Bath in Britain are two of Europe's famous spa towns. Spa water is thought to be good for you because of the minerals it contains, but it often tastes unpleasant.

.... is a method of treating people with particular diseases or injuries by making them exercise in water. It enables patients to exercise without straining their bodies and is a recommended form of treatment for arthritis.

The English generally prefer .... because they think it's cleaner. In fact, the reverse is the case because in a bath you lie in dirty water. In the time of Shakespeare, it was common for people to only have one bath a year. Fortunately, habits have changed a lot since then!

They say that *you can lead a horse to water but you can't make it drink* because ....
They also say *blood is thicker than water* to indicate the importance of family ties.

Everything you always wanted to know about Water (Version B)

Water is the common name applied to the liquid state of the hydrogen-oxygen compound. Pure water is an odourless, tasteless liquid with a bluish tint. However, this colour can only be detected in ....

Water is the only substance that occurs at ordinary temperatures in all three states of matter – as a solid, a liquid and a gas. It covers three-quarters of the surface of the earth in the form of swamps, lakes, rivers and oceans. It is also the major constituent of living matter - from 50 to 90 percent of the weight of living organisms is water.

The world's five oceans, the main areas of sea, ...…… ……………........................... .And the longest river is the Mississippi-Missouri.

………….. is the science concerned with the distribution of water on the earth, its physical and chemical reactions with other naturally occurring substances, and its relation to life on earth.

Rain is the precipitation of liquid drops of water. The world's heaviest average rainfall, about 10,922 mm per year, occurs at Cherrapunji, in northeastern India, where moisture-laden air from the Bay of Bengal is forced to rise over the Khasi Hills of Assam State. A long period when there is little or no rain is known as …………...

Clouds are a condensed form of atmospheric moisture consisting of small water droplets or tiny ice crystals and rainfall is dependent on their formation. More than 100 different kinds of clouds are distinguishable and the development of the high-altitude plane has introduced a species of artificial clouds known as contrails. These are formed from ………………………………………………............……………………….. They say that *every cloud has a silver lining* to suggest that even in bad things you can always find something good.

A spa is a fashionable town where water comes out of the ground and people come to drink or lie in it because they think it will improve their health. Baden Baden in Germany and Bath in Britain are two of Europe's famous spa towns. Spa

water is thought to be good for you because ....
.........................., but it often tastes unpleasant.

Hydrotherapy is a method of treating people with particular
diseases or injuries by making them exercise in water. It
enables patients to .... and is
a recommended form of treatment for arthritis.

The English generally prefer a bath to a shower because they
think it's cleaner. In fact, the reverse is the case because in a
bath you lie in dirty water. In the time of Shakespeare, it was
common for people to .... Fortunately,
habits have changed a lot since then!

They say that *you can lead a horse to water but you can't make it
drink* because people have to learn from their own experiences. They also say .... to indicate the
importance of family ties.

Bibliography

Berman, M. (2002). A *Multiple Intelligences Road to an ELT
Classroom*. Carmarthen: Crown House Publishing.

Gardner, H. (1983). *Frames of Mind. The Theory of Multiple
Intelligences*, New York: Basic Books.

Gardner, H. (1993). *Multiple Intelligences. The Theory in Practice*.
New York: Basic Books.

Gardner, H. (1999). *Intelligence Reframed. Multiple Intelligences for
the 21st Century*. New York: Basic Books.

Gardner, H. (2006). *Multiple Intelligences*: New Horizons. New
York: Basic Books.

18

Handle with Care!

WORDS CONFUSED & WORDS MISUSED: The learners can work individually on these exercises and then pair up to compare their answers. This way of working appeals to those students who are highly intrapersonal and prefer to work on their own initially before getting together with others. Alternatively, the learners can work in pairs from the outset, and then get together in groups of four to see if they can reach a consensus. This method of working not only appeals to those members of the group who have strong interpersonal skills, but also reduces the likelihood of errors.

Instead of merely asking the students to find the correct answers, you could also ask them to consider why the alternatives are inappropriate. And for homework or follow-up work in class, you could ask them to make sentences of their own with the words they had problems with, to show they now know how to use them. They can then exchange these with another member of the class, and try to correct each other's work before you look through the sentences and check them.

Choose the correct answer from each pair of alternatives:

1. Three of the computers are beyond repair / reparations and the time has come to replace them.
2. Industrial relations/relationships in this company are at an all-time low, and we clearly need to address this issue before the situation gets any worse.
3. Hopefully the worst of our problems are behind us and it should be high flying / plain sailing from now on.

4. You would be breaking the law if you went ahead and did that, and it is really not worth / worthy of the risk.

5. If I invest all my savings in a fixed / set term deposit account, what would the interest rate be?

6. As long as you play your cards right, you will find yourself in a line for / in line for promotion very soon

7. Financially, I'm in a bit of a fix and I was wandering / wondering whether you could help me out and borrow / lend me some, just to tide / tie me over for the next few days until I get paid.

8. I would if I could but I'm afraid I can't. I'm a bit short myself at a / the moment, to say / tell you a / the true / truth.

9. In view of / With a view to all the hard work you have put in over the last few months, we feel your promotion is fully justified.

10. Despite / In spite all our efforts, a little / little has been achieved I am afraid to say and in truth we are really no better off than when we first started.

11. You really need to be more careful because if what you have to say is misconstrued, it could well cause an offence / offences.

12. We trust you will find the proposal to be of interest, and hope to hear from you by return of post / by the return of the post.

13. Unfortunately economic / economical hardship seems to have become a way of life / living these days for the majority of us, and making ends meet is a constant struggle.

14. You seem to have got yourself into a real mess and there is absolutely no way I can bail / bale you out of this. A / The truth is that nobody could.

15. On balance / In the balance we feel you did / made a better impression at the interview than the other applicant, that / which is why, at / in the end we decided to offer you the job.

ANSWERS: 1 repair 2 relations 3 plain sailing 4 worth 5 fixed 6 in line for 7 wondering / lend / tie 8 the / tell / truth 9 In view of 10 Despite / little 11 an offence 12 by return of post 13 economic / life 14 bail / The 15 On balance / made / which / in

Choose the correct answer from each pair of alternatives:

1. I am not convinced that the location for the store is really suitable as it is a bit off a / the beaten track and there / it is unlikely to be any passing business / trade in an area like that.
2. If you are in need of advice / advise, you had better / ought to consult a solicitor and, if you are lucky, you might even be allowed / entitled to legal aid. It depends on how much you are currently / presently earning.
3. I can assure / ensure you that you have absolutely nothing at all to worry about as I have the situation in / on hand, and of that there should be no doubt.
4. To all in tents / intents and purposes I am a language teacher, but in practice / practise all I do is entertain my students with bad jokes.
5. Although / Despite I rarely receive any praise for the work I produce, I still manage to enjoy my job somehow.
6. It is time we did / made a stand against this kind of behaviour at / in the workplace because it is totally unacceptable in this day and age / time.
7. I would not raise / rise my hopes too high if I were you - they still have a the number of other candidates to interview, some of whom / what are a lot better qualified than you.
8. You seem to have an awful lot on your dish / plate at the moment, with there being so many staff off ill / sick, so I think I had better leave you to get on with it.
9. I have been out of my head / mind with worry over you.

Where on earth have you been all this time?

10. We have a lot riding on this deal so please do you best to assure / ensure you manage to pull it off. For if we loose / lose the contract for any reason, I hate thinking / to think what the consequences might be.

11. We are not home and dry / safe just yet and we still have a long distance / way to go before we can claim to be well and truly on the road / path to recovery.

12. I wish it / there was something I could do or say to make you change / to change your mind but I seem to be banging / beating my head against a brick wall here and I just have to accept a / the fact.

13. It / There is absolutely no excuse for poor service on flights, especially if you travel first / the first class. It is just plain / plane annoying when this happens and it really makes my / the blood boil.

14. You have really been most / the most kind and I would like you to know that all the efforts you have done / made on my behalf have been greatly appreciated / appreciative.

15. The announcement is often made on London Underground that there is a good service on all lines when it is clear to everyone waiting that this is not the case. I find myself irritated / irritating beyond belief / beliefs when this happens and it annoys me intensely / intensively.

ANSWERS: 1 the / there / trade 2 advice / ought / entitled / currently 3 assure / in 4 intents / practice 5 Although 6 made / in / age 7 raise / whom 8 plate / sick 9 mind 10 ensure / lose / to think 11 dry / way / road 12 there / change / banging / the 13 There / first / plain / my 14 most / made / appreciated 15 irritated / belief / intensely

***

Nouns that are countable in other languages are often uncountable in English, meaning they cannot be used with the indefinite article or made plural. Here are a couple of exercises that feature the uncountable nouns learners often make mistakes with that you might like to make use of in class.

UNCOUNTABLE NOUNS (nouns that are never used with the indefinite article): Use each uncountable noun in the following list once only to complete the sentences you will find below: accommodation / assistance / denial / experience / fame / feedback / hospitality / information / legislation / money / progress / recognition / research / resistance / satisfaction / service / training

1. Despite all our efforts to trace what happened to the _____ that has gone missing, unfortunately it still remains unaccounted for.
2. Although considerable _____ has been made over the last twelve months, we still have a long way to go before we can say the company is financially sound once again.
3. It is high time you received some _____ for all the work you have been doing behind the scenes.
4. Your _____ has truly been overwhelming and I can safely say I have never been looked after anywhere so well before.
5. Should you need any _____, all you need to do is to contact me.
6. As you can see you are heavily outnumbered, so any _____ on your part would just be futile.
7. No previous _____ of this kind of work is required, because full _____ will be provided.
8. Any _____ you have for me on the presentation I gave

would be very much appreciated.

9. _____ unequivocally shows, beyond any shadow of a doubt, that cigarettes can seriously damage your health, even if you smoke a low tar brand.

10. I wish there was some way we could find out more _____ about the subject, but hardly anything seems to be known about it.

11. Unfortunately the _____ provided for the delegates attending the Conference was far from ideal but it was all that was available.

12. There is no need to leave any tip as _____ has already been included in the bill.

13. I wonder what you are looking for in life – fortune or _____, or maybe be neither. Perhaps something else is more important to you – job _____, for example.

14. The _____ aimed at improving industrial relations that the government introduced has unfortunately proved to be ineffective and alternative measures will now need to be considered.

15. Your inability to accept the situation you find yourself in would suggest that you are in _____.

ANSWERS: 1 money 2 progress 3 recognition 4 hospitality 5 assistance 6 resistance 7 experience / training 8 feedback 9 research 10 information 11 accommodation 12 service 13 fame / satisfaction 14 legislation 15 denial

UNCOUNTABLE NOUNS: Use each uncountable noun in the following list once only to complete the sentences you will find below: air / assistance / baggage / compensation / evidence / furniture / hair / information / medicine / nonsense / paper / rubbish / stress / trouble / value / water

1. All this worry over the future of the company is making

my _____ turn grey.

2. Please be assured that your _____ is kept strictly confidential and that we take your privacy very seriously.

3. Take a dose of this _____ three times a day and you will soon feel better.

4. Apart from the fact that all the _____ needs replacing, the room could also do with a new coat of paint.

5. You really must try to be less wasteful. Most of what you regard as _____ and have thrown in the bin can actually be recycled.

6. There is no appreciable difference in quality between the two products. It is simply that one is far cheaper than the other and so offers consumers better _____.

7. If you are going to make a serious accusation like that, you will need to produce some _____ to support your case.

8. In times of _____ you find out who your real friends are and it can come as quite a surprise.

9. I have been under a lot of _____ recently and could really do with a break from it all.

10. If you require special _____ in the airport, you need to advise the airline prior to travel and they will make special arrangements for you.

11. Airlines will not provide monetary _____ for flights that are delayed or cancelled for reasons beyond their control.

12. Each fare-paying passenger is allowed to carry a certain amount of _____. However, the amount you are allowed and how much you have to pay for extra items and additional weight differs depending on your destination and the airline you are flying.

13. What a load of rubbish! I have never heard such _____ before!

14. Trees suck carbon dioxide from the _____, cutting the level of greenhouse gas in the atmosphere. By recycling _____, you can help to save them.
15. Office emails can land you in hot _____. Sending an email in error can even cost you your job.

ANSWERS: 1 hair 2 information 3 medicine 4 furniture 5 rubbish 6 value 7 evidence 8 trouble 9 stress 10 assistance 11 compensation 12 baggage 13 nonsense 14 air / paper 15 water

Learner involvement is frequently at its best when the student is perplexed and confused, but not yet frustrated. "Positive dissatisfaction" can be used to engage learners at peak levels of motivation and understanding, and you can purposely put participants into a state of controlled frustration in order to develop better quality thinking, patience and mental toughness. For this reason, instead of attempting a conventional form of grammar review, you might like to consider making use of a 'How much do you know about...?' type questionnaire, like the two examples presented below. The learners' embarrassment at their poor results will act as a spur to further study and help them to overcome their initial complacency. Moreover, as such activities entail problem-solving, they provide an ideal way of catering for the logical-mathematical Intelligence type:

How much do you know about Idioms? Decide whether the following statements are true or false and give reasons for the choices you make:

1. All phrasal verbs are idioms and all idioms are phrasal verbs.
2. Idioms are a separate part of the language you can choose either to use or omit.
3. Idioms can be defined as colloquial expressions.

4. Idioms are fixed expressions that cannot be changed.
5. Words with grammatical functions can be used idiomatically.
6. All proverbs are idioms.
7. All proverbs are sayings.
8. You are more likely to find idioms in quality newspapers than in the tabloids or popular press.
9. All idioms, by definition, are cliches.
10. One of the problems for language learners is that idioms tend to be culturally bound.

***

All the answers are false except for numbers five, seven and ten. To find out the reasons, take a look at the explanations below:

1. False. All phrasal verbs are idioms but not all idioms are phrasal verbs. Certain idioms contain no verbs. You appeared "out of the blue" and caught me by surprise, for example.
2. False. They form an essential part of the general vocabulary of English and "I hope you get the point and see what I mean" to give you two examples!
3. False. They can appear in formal style and in slang, in poetry or in the language of Shakespeare and the Bible.
4. False. Not all idioms are fixed. Sometimes the tense of the verb can be changed: "I'm going to have forty winks" or "I had forty winks" And sometimes the adjective can be varied: "You'd better keep a careful/close/sharp/watchful eye on her"
5. True. An example is the use of SHALL to offer help or to make a suggestion: "Shall I carry the bag for you?" or "Shall we have an early night for a change?"
6. False. All proverbs can be used idiomatically but a

number of proverbs are also statements of fact and easily understood in their literal meaning. For example: "If at first you don't succeed, try, try, try again"

7. True. In the "Advanced Learner's Dictionary" a proverb is defined as "a short well-known sentence that states a general truth about life or gives advice" and a saying is defined as "a well-known phrase, expression or proverb"

8. False. You are far more likely to find idioms in the tabloids.

9. False. According to the "Advanced Learner's Dictionary" a cliché is a phrase "which is used so often that it is no longer interesting, effective or relevant" If this definition could be applied to all idioms, there would be little point in teaching them!

10. True. A good example of this is "as cool as a cucumber" The connection between cool and cucumber is far from obvious. However, every native speaker will naturally put the two words together. In English we say "as stubborn as a mule" whereas in Turkish the association is "as stubborn as a pig" In English we say "as strong as an ox" whereas in Dutch the association is "as strong as a bear"

***

How much do you know about the Gerund and the Infinitive?
Decide whether the following statements are true or false and give reasons for the choices you make:

1. TO is always followed by the infinitive of a verb.
2. MAKE is the only verb that is followed by an object and the plain infinitive.
3. Modal verbs are always followed by the plain infinitive.
4. The verb TO START can be followed by the gerund or the

TO infinitive but with a change of meaning.

5. The gerund can be used as the subject of a sentence but not the TO infinitive.

6. Verbs expressing likes and dislikes can be followed by the gerund or the TO infinitive without any change of meaning.

7. The following sentence is grammatically incorrect: "I suggest that she buy an English-English dictionary."

8. The following sentences both have the same meaning: "He helped me carry the luggage" and "He helped me to carry the luggage."

9. The verb LET has no passive form.

10. Both the gerund and the infinitive are defective because they have no perfect forms to talk about actions earlier in time.

***

All the statements are false except for number eight. To find out the reasons, take a look at the explanations below:

1. False. "I'm looking forward to meeting you" and "He confessed to murdering his mother-in-law" are two of many examples when TO is followed by the gerund.

2. False. LET is also followed by an object and the plain infinitive: My parents never used to let me smoke.

3. False. OUGHT is followed by the TO infinitive: You ought to buy yourself an English-English dictionary.

4. False. The verb TO START can be followed by the gerund or the TO infinitive and the two forms are inter-changeable: When did you start studying/to study English?

5. False. The gerund is more commonly used as the subject of a sentence but the TO infinitive can also be used: To be

or not to be, that is the question.

6. False. Verbs expressing likes and dislikes are followed by the gerund when talking in general and followed by the TO infinitive to refer to particular events: Do you like dancing? Would you like to dance with me?

7. False. The verb TO SUGGEST can be followed by the gerund or a THAT clause: The guide suggested visiting the Tower of London. The guide suggested (that) the tourist (should) visit the Tower of London.

8. True. HELP can be followed by an object and the plain or the TO infinitive without any change of meaning.

9. False. "The prisoners were let out of their cells twice a day" is an example of the verb used in the passive. However, when LET SOMEONE DO is used to express permission there is no passive form of the verb: My boss let me go home early.

10. False."Joan of Arc is said to have been a witch" and "The suspect confessed to having committed the crime" are examples of the perfect forms.

Appendix (i): Telling Tales to Teenagers by Wayne Rimmer

Many of the contributions in this volume are testimony to the power of storytelling. What should be clear from the range and variety of stories offered is that there is something for everyone in a storytelling methodology. Younger learners are no exception. Beginning with the routine of bedtime stories and going on to the study of 'serious' literature at school, stories are a crucial part of a child's cognitive and socio-cultural development. There may be the objection that children are reading less in this technological age, that stories cannot compete with the attractions of a 24 hour 3D video culture. However, the fact is that technology provides an even greater stimulus to children's imagination. Modern children are surrounded by information and their natural curiosity for knowledge makes them incredibly receptive to channels for sorting and filtering that information. In other words this is the perfect context for storytelling, as stories, whether fables or jokes, are surely the oldest and most tested way of making sense of a world which has always seemed bizarre and confusing at any stage of human evolution.

Stories then need little justification in the young learner classroom. 'Young learner' covers a wide age-range. There are many pre-school children studying English who will probably go on to study English right through their period of compulsory education, and beyond. ELT coursebooks and resource materials are very coy about giving target age-groups, for marketing reasons, but the consensus seems to be that a young learner is someone who has not finished school yet. There are many story-telling materials available for young learners. For example, books for pre-school children often come with video stories and even puppet characters. Curiously, the primary age-group, ages up to 11 years old, is much better-served than teenagers. True, much adult material could be used successfully with teenagers (there are many examples in this volume) but the mainstream publishers have not done much to target teenagers specifically.

Below are three speculative reasons for this with their rationale.

1. Teenagers are not interested in stories anymore.

Adolescents are keen to distance themselves from children and do not want any association with what are seen as childhood interests. The worse thing for any teenager is to be seen to be childish. In other words, stories are not cool enough.

2. It is too difficult to find stories which appeal to teenagers.

The teenage period is associated with tremendous physiological and mental changes. There is also a great deal of peer pressure and crises of confidence, stoked up by advertising and the popular media. These forces make the teenage market unstable in that teenagers' tastes and preferences are constantly changing as they desperately seek a fresh identity. In this atmosphere, it is nigh near impossible to predict which stories will work.

3. Teenagers should concentrate on formal language study or exam preparation.

We live in an age which demands accountability. On the oft-cited premise that we tend to value what we can measure, syllabi and tests stress discrete language points so that knowledge can be compared and ultimately judged. Teenagers are not exempt from this process and school curricula typically place great emphasis on formal assessment. There is simply no time and place for methodologies which do not offer quantifiable learning goals.

These points do generalise the issues, for instance, it is not true that formal assessment precludes storytelling. Even some public exams, e.g. the Cambridge ESOL *Certificate of Advanced English*, include a set book option, which encourages the study and enjoyment of narrative. However, the three points do relate to real concerns, so they are addressed in turn.

1. Teenagers are not interested in stories anymore.

There are stories and stories. Teenagers will not react well to anything perceived as childish but they will enjoy a tale they can relate to. A classic example is urban legends, those bizarre and whacky stories of alligators in the New York subways, Kentucky fried rats, etc. Teenagers love this mix of the grisly and implausible because it highlights the many contradictions in their own lives. The trick is to find the right story, which leads to the next point.

2. It is too difficult to find stories which appeal to teenagers.

Who is doing the finding? If it is a middle-aged teacher who hates teenage classes, or, worse, the writer of a global coursebook trying to make the book as commercially successful in as many countries as possible, the chances are that the story selected will lack resonance. As the class teacher, you are in a much stronger position to target your teenagers' needs. It's your class so get to know them and what stories they like. Even better, get your teenagers to bring in or make their own stories. As a simple example, for homework, ask each teenager to come to class with a joke in English.

3. Teenagers should concentrate on formal language study or exam preparation.

Stories offer an extended and authentic context for presenting, practicing and producing new language. As shown in the second activity below, it is easy to teach grammar through stories. In fact, stories are an ideal vehicle for language work because they personalise the target language so effectively. The trick is to make the goals transparent to students, and parents: 'We're listening to this story because we need to practise more prepositions.' If you have a very tight syllabus to deliver you may try to tell yourself that you do not have time for stories. Think again because almost certainly the converse is true - you do not have time not to tell stories.

The proof of the pudding is in the eating so below are two sample storytelling activities for teenagers. However, as said above, the real skill in telling stories to teenagers is to select material and tasks which suit their needs and interests. This is more work for you than asking the learners to go to page 73 in the coursebook but teenagers will definitely appreciate the effort you make and respond accordingly. As any teacher of teenagers knows, the highs and lows of teaching this age-group are extreme, but the right story massively increases the chance of a very positive learning experience.

Rumpelstiltskin

Level: B1 +
Topic: fairy-tale
Language focus: mixed
Skills focus: listening, speaking, sentence writing
Time: 60 minutes

Procedure
1. Learners complete names quiz in pairs.
2. Go through the answers in class and surprise learners by

giving Rumpelstiltskin as an answer for question 5.

3. Tell the story using the story skeleton: use gesture, intonation and drama to enhance the meaning. Remind learners before you begin telling the story that they will have to listen carefully as there are comprehension questions afterwards. (It takes learners a few minutes usually to realize that the questions are nothing to do with the story as told!)

4. Learners complete the questions individually and then ask each other.

5. Questions 9, 10, 11 are extra silly questions for learners to come up with: the sillier, the better.

Names quiz

How much do you like your name? Give it a grade from 1 – 5.

_____

What is the surname of the Queen of England?

_____

English people have 3 names. Why?

_____

Sasha in Russian could be a man or a woman's name. Can you think of an English name with dual gender?

_____

What is the name of the highest mountain in Britain?

_____

Which one of the following is not a traditional British name?
Alice, Carmel, Helen, Irene, Vanessa, Vera, Wendy?

_____

Think of a man's name beginning with R and write it down.

_____

(Answers)

2. Windsor

3. A Roman tradition.

4. Lesley, Alex, Jo …
5. Ben Nevis
6. Wendy (coined by Barrie for the girl in Peter Pan)
7. Robert, Richard, Randy… Rumpelstiltskin.

Rumpelstiltskin – story skeleton

Miller has beautiful daughter. King rides by, notices daughter. Miller boasts of how beautiful, clever, strong, etc daughter is. He adds that his daughter can spin straw into gold. King decides to test miller, takes girl to his castle. He puts girl in small room full of straw and says, Spin this into gold by tomorrow morning or you die!' then leaves.

Girl distraught. Little green man knocks and enters room. He promises to spin the straw into gold if girl gives him her ring. She agrees and the straw is spun into gold. Dwarf leaves room, King returns and is amazed. This time he puts girl in a bigger room full of straw and says, Spin this into gold by tomorrow morning or you die!' then leaves.

Girl distraught. Little green man knocks and enters room. He promises to spin the straw into gold if girl gives him her necklace. She agrees and the straw is spun into gold. Dwarf leaves room, King returns and is amazed. This time he puts girl in a huge room full of straw and says, Spin this into gold by tomorrow morning and I'll marry you. If you don't, you die!' then leaves.

Girl distraught. Little green man knocks and enters room. He promises to spin the straw into gold if girl promises him her first-born baby. She agrees and the straw is spun into gold. Dwarf leaves room, King returns and is amazed. The King marries the girl.

One year later the now Queen has a baby. Dwarf returns to claim the baby. Queen distraught. Dwarf says Queen can only keep baby if she guesses his name. The Queen tries all the names under the sun but in vain. The dwarf gives her 3 days to find out his name.

Queen sends messengers all over Europe and Asia to find names. They return with a big list but none of them are the dwarf's name. 2 days left.

Queen sends messengers all over Africa and America to find names. They return with a big list but none of them are the dwarf's name. 1 day left.

Queen in despair. She is walking in the forest when she sees something strange. The little man dancing around the fire and singing a song.

'Oh let me play my little game,

For no one can guess my name.

That my name is secret, I have no fear,

Of Rumpelstitlskin, you will never hear!'

Queen delighted. Meets dwarf that evening. He demands baby. Queen reveals the name. Rumpelstiltskin turns white and flies out of the window, never to be seen again.

Rumpelstiltskin – questions

	Me	Partner
1. What did Rumpelstiltskin have for breakfast?		
2. What do dwarves do in their free time?		
3. Where did Rumpelstiltskin go in his last vacation?		
4. Why are dwarves always the bad guys in fairy-tales?		
5. How does Rumpelstiltskin spin so quickly?		
6. Would Rumpelstiltskin be a good father? Why (not)?		

7. What is Rumpelstiltskin's
kitchen like?
8. What would you buy
Rumpelstiltskin for
Christmas?
9.
10.
11.

Are you a model student?

Level: B2 +
Topic: school / student life
Language focus: collocations, present continuous + adverbs of frequency.
Skills focus: speaking, sentence writing
Time: 60 minutes

Procedure
1. Ask class about things they like and don't like about school.
2. Learners do collocations quiz individually.
3. Learners quiz each other.
4. Go through collocations as a class.
5. Learners do both role-plays, swapping roles so there is a total of four speaking tasks.
6. Explain grammar point using the model sentence in the role-play and set up the writing activity.
7. Class discussion about annoying habits.

Extension activity for vocabulary building
Learners make their own quizzes in groups using collocations they have found in monolingual dictionaries.

1. Collocations quiz

Are you a **model student**?

1. You get home late and tired but you have an English essay to write. What do you do?
a. Go to bed and hope this is all a bad dream
b. Drink two cups of **super-strong coffee** and get to work
c. Download something from the internet

2. What would be an ideal weekend for you?
a. Not leaving your bed
b. Spending some **quality time** in the library
c. Earning some extra money so you can buy some **trendy clothes**

3. What kind of people do you always sit next to in class?
a. beautiful ones
b. ones that won't distract you too much
c. ones that know all the answers

4. You have a test tomorrow and you are in a panic. What do you do?
a. Write all the answers on the back of your hand
b. Stay up all night revising
c. **Soak in** the **bath** and go to bed early

5. You get a bad mark in the test. How do you react?
a. Feel relieved – you haven't been **kicked out of** the **class** yet.
b. Study twice as hard in the future
c. **Complain bitterly** to your teacher that the test was unfair

6. What is the best way to learn new vocabulary?
a. With **close friends** and maybe a few beers (don't tell my dad!)

b. Test yourself every evening.

c. Write new words on the wallpaper in your apartment

7. What kind of parties do you like?

a. **Wild parties** where anything can happen

b. Quiet gatherings of **like-minded people**

c. Parties where the food and drink are free

Answers

Lots of As. You are the student from hell. I'm amazed you came today!

Lots of Bs. You are either a **model student** or a **compulsive liar**.

Lots of Cs. You have a practical approach and should do well.

2. Speaking role-plays

A.
You are a teacher. You want to ask your student why he/she has not been to classes for three weeks.

B.
You are a student. You have not been to class for three weeks because it has been difficult to to get out of bed early. Your teacher wants to see you - think of a good excuse to tell him / her.

A.
You are a teacher. You have noticed that your student is always falling asleep in class. Speak to him / her about this.

B.
You are a student. You often fall asleep in class because your teacher is so boring! Oh no, now your teacher wants to talk to you!

3. Grammar tip

You have noticed that your student is always falling asleep in class.

We use the present continuous and *always* or *constantly* to complain about bad habits and tendencies that annoy us.

Jane is constantly complaining!
It's always raining in Manchester!

Write down five things that annoy you about yourself, your teachers and friends.

1. I'm always losing my homework!
2.
3.
4.
5.

Appendix (ii): Exploring Choice Theory
by Mojca Belak

The idea that people can really choose their own behaviour, their own reactions, can at first seem strange. The widely accepted view is that it is *others* who make a person happy, sad, jealous, and so on. This is deeply imbedded in the language also, which is why the accepted way of expressing the cause of one's anger is with statements such as *You broke my heart*, or *You know how to make me cross*, and the like. But the truth is that it is the person themselves who chooses that very behaviour. Different people are more or less successful in preventing others from interfering with their feelings; indeed, the art of controlling one's own feelings and reactions can be learned, mostly through a lot of practice and many mistakes along the way, which is where personal growth overlaps with Choice Theory.

Some basics

The founder of Choice theory is William Glasser, an American psychologist, who is also the father of Quality School projects growing rapidly around the world. Choice Theory differs from other psychologies in that it rejects the commonly accepted view that outside events influence somebody's behaviour. Instead it stresses that people can and should take control of their own lives and stop trying to control others. Basically, there are two general statements at the very core of Choice theory: *I cannot change others* and *I can only choose* my *own behaviour*. Knowing more about Choice theory can help to solve every-day problems and can deepen the awareness of how people interact.

People like to think that they cannot control their feelings. The common belief is that feelings either happen or are triggered from the outside by other people or situations. The following story explores whether such a thinking frame really works in practice.

Peter was perfectly happy when he drove his brand new car for the first time. It had taken him years of scrimping and saving to afford it and now he was on top of the world. But just when he stopped at the red light, another car hit him from behind. Peter simply couldn't believe what had happened. He could feel his blood boiling as he switched off the engine, got out of the car and waited for the driver of the other car to show his or her face. In his mind he was already rehearsing offensive words and phrases he was going to shout at the careless driver.

Points to think about:
Even though Peter was cross, do you think his mood could change if he found out that the other car was driven by

a. an attractive young woman
b. a big uncompromising bully
c. a frightened spotted teenager
d. a confused middle-aged scientist?

Peter's reaction would most probably be different in any of the above situations, which proves that people can indeed control their behaviour.

Here's another example:

When Eva, my friend's daughter, was a toddler and started having tantrums, she carried them out very dramatically. She threw herself down and banged her small fists on the floor. Bored with this performance, which she was carrying out in the hall, her father once closed the door leading to the living room where he was sitting. Eva was left without an audience, so she stopped yelling, got on her feet, went to the living room door, opened it and then returned to the hall, threw herself on the floor again and continued her tantrum. That way the girl showed that she was in perfect control of her feelings.

Interestingly, pop songs and soap operas often lead people to think that it is others who control their own feelings and reactions. Such a thinking frame alienates the person from their source; instead of looking inside for clues and taking an opportunity to change something about themselves, people blame others for their own misfortune. This way they miss great opportunity to develop.

People always have a choice. Imagine you've just had some bad news. How do you react? You can get upset, you can go to people who you know will give you support, you can spend most of your time thinking about it. Or, alternatively, you can focus on something more pleasant that you are currently doing in life or do something active like going for a walk. And these are only some out of many possible options...

Consider you have fully accepted that you are in charge of your own actions and reactions and have started believing that nobody can influence or change you unless you want to change. What does this mean in the context of teaching? Could it be that students will only learn from the teacher if they want that, or looking at this from another angle, could it mean that there is no way the teacher can make students learn if they are disinterested in the subject, school or the teacher herself?

Quality world

From a very early age onwards people build their own quality worlds in their minds. In them they store images, pictures or emotions which bring the feelings of well being or pleasure. A baby would start its unique collection of pictures with images of the mother, her lap, feeding, other family members, and so on. Later in life other actions, people, objects, feelings, etc. are gradually added, and the person will strive to live the pictures from their quality world. They will try out different behaviour to make them come true. Their feeling of happiness or achievement will greatly depend on the quality world they have built over the years. If somebody puts family life high on the quality world list, they will try to reach this goal, and achieving it will be very important for them. If they should fail in this respect, they would feel much more upset and negative than someone who also doesn't have a family but has never included the picture of a family in their quality world.

If a child has a good relationship with its parents and the parents think that going to school, working hard and getting a good education is important, then the child will soon put all these ideas into his or her quality world. It won't be difficult to go to school and work hard even when they don't feel like it. Most teachers keep the idea of school and obtaining a degree in their quality worlds: some have taken this idea (picture) over from their parents, who they trusted, while others placed it there themselves later in life.

Points to think about:
What pictures do you have in your quality world?
What do you think your favourite student has in his/her quality world?
What pictures do you think your most difficult student has in his/her quality world?

Of course, not all learners have placed school in their quality world, which is what teachers, with their different quality worlds, may find difficult to understand. If school is not in a child's quality world, then the child will not strive to achieve what is in this picture. Very often the people who are in the quality world of such a child - his or her family, friends, or neighbours, don't have school in their quality worlds either.

Trying to teach somebody who likes neither the teacher nor the subject is impossible. The teacher doesn't have control over her students and cannot make them learn unless they themselves want to.

Teachers cannot make students learn

The only way for the teacher to succeed in such a situation is, according to Glasser, to try and get into the students' quality world. In order to achieve this, the teacher has to be accepted by the students as a human being, not only as a teacher. Shouting, humiliating, threatening and punishing students will definitely not get the teacher into students' quality worlds. Many problematic children lack an understanding, warm personality in their lives and if the teacher, instead of being a figure of authority, strives to be more humane, chances are that she will be accepted, liked, and respected. All this opens the door to the students' quality world.

The following story told by spiritual Master Rajinder Singh further illustrates this point:

The Power of a Teacher's Love

Once there was a schoolteacher who was celebrating her eightieth birthday. The teacher had spent many years teaching in an inner-city school. Before coming to her, many of the students at her school had been involved in antisocial behaviours. But, as the teacher worked there, people noticed a dramatic change in her students. Many of them grew up to be good citizens. Many went on to become doctors, lawyers, teachers, skilled technicians, and businesspeople. People noticed the difference that this teacher made in many of the lives of her students.

It was no wonder that on her eightieth birthday her former students arrived to pay their respects and offer their gratitude to her for all that she had done for them.

The newspapers heard about this grand birthday party and sent a reporter to cover the story. The reporter who interviewed her asked, "What was the secret to your success as a teacher?"

The teacher replied, "As I look around at the young teachers who graduate today, I find that they are focused on the skills in their profession. When I look back, I realize that when I started teaching, all I had to give was love!" (Singh: 2006: 72-73)

Students like teachers who are kind and caring, and above all, who are interested in them. Listening, too, is very important – a teacher who talks to her students and takes into consideration what they say, also has a chance to get into their quality worlds. Sometimes it is good to ask students for some advice because they may have answers the teacher would never think of. The next example is from my own teaching experience:

A few years ago a student in my class was particularly chatty and practically never stopped talking. I tried to attract her attention in different ways, but nothing worked, so once I explained to her that I found her chatting in class disturbing and asked her what she would advise me to do about it. She came up with some fresh ideas I would never have thought of and which, not surprisingly, worked.

The four psychological needs

According to Choice Theory, every human being has five universal needs. Apart from the very basic, physiological need to survive (eat, drink, sleep, multiply) each person has four basic psychological needs: love and belonging, power, freedom and fun. Glasser claims that these needs are driven by our genes and since all human beings are members of the same species, all people have the same genetic needs. However, what makes each person unique is how pronounced these needs are. While one person may need a lot of love and primarily wants to satisfy their need to belong, another is more power-hungry, and yet another needs more freedom than the first two. From a very early age on, a person always knows how they feel, and strives to feel good. And "just as a northern migrating bird must always attempt to fly south for the winter, we, too, must attempt to live our lives in ways that we believe will best satisfy our needs" (Glasser 1998b: 46).

Love and belonging

The most important of the four is the need to be loved, love and belong because people seem to feel happy and content only if they are close to those they care about. This need is not only about finding a special person in one's life. It encompasses the need to be close to those a person lets into their life on a more intimate level. A good relationship with parents or siblings will grant the fulfilment of this need in early childhood, while later in life it will be satisfied in relationships with friends, maybe a spouse, children, teachers, trainers, spiritual teachers as well as belonging to various groups – from friends who regularly meet at the pub or over a coffee to members of the same club or association. No matter how old a person is, if they are rejected by their family, friends or colleagues, they feel unhappy.

Ideally, a teacher should therefore be kind, caring and deeply interested in their students as well as in the subject they teach. A successful teacher should be able to listen to the students and sometimes ask their advice.

However, having a good relationship with students isn't always well accepted, as Glasser (1998b: 58) points out in his description of problems that a teacher who wants to lead and not boss students around, will encounter: "The lead-teacher will also be criticized for caring too much and told that too much personal involvement is unprofessional. She will be admonished to keep the state assessment tests in mind and to fragment the subject so that students will do better on these tests, even though this approach fails to capture the attention of over half the students. She will quickly learn that in schools (as well as in a world) dominated by boss-managers, she will be unpopular for what she believes and especially for what she does. She will see many boss-teachers failing miserably, but still most of those who run the system will continue to support what the boss-teachers do as right and criticize her as wrong."

Power

The need for power is closely connected with respect and self-worth. In a relationship power means that I can do things my way, for example squeeze the toothpaste in the middle of the tube and not at the end, and I am not criticised for it. According to Choice theory, many relationships break down not because there is no love in them any longer but because spouses never learn how to share power. The need for power is interesting in that bossing other people around usually results in the need for more power, not less. Some people feel empowered when they have a lot of money, others exercise their power by shouting at others, insulting or even beating them.

A teacher who badly needs power is usually distant, cold and controlling. They will often resort to criticising students in many different ways. Any comments on students' mental (dis)abilities or shouting at them are markers of this need. Threatening or punishing students are also indicators of a power-hungry teacher.

However, people are different and in a situation where one person needs their ego to be massaged a lot, somebody else working under exactly the same circumstances and with the same learners may not feel the need to show their power at all. Teachers who aspire to leading instead of coercing do not overuse their power when they teach.

Freedom

People find freedom so important that some are even ready to fight or kill for it. In everyday life, freedom lies in most decisions and actions: we choose where we live, how and who with. It is in the human nature to strive for freedom, which is why people tend to break rules which make no sense. In a teaching situation students who do not feel free because of (too many) rules lose interest and may even become disruptive.

If I find myself in a situation where I am forced to do something, I will more often than not feel the need to rebel or at least resort to criticising. A while ago almost one hundred lorry drivers blocked the busiest streets of my town during the morning rush hour as part of their protest. That way they exercised their power, which, admittedly, they have, especially when they are behind the wheel. But while showing off their power, lorry drivers took away the freedom of many people who had to either go to work or do their errands at that time. And even though the lorry drivers' ingenious plan to attract attention did not directly affect me, I found myself secretly longing for those long lost times when people still threw bad eggs and rotten tomatoes at those they didn't like.

Points to think about:
How do you react when you think your need for freedom is not satisfied?
Do you keep this reaction inside or do you bring it into the open?

If students are forbidden too many things, if the lists of don'ts vastly exceed the do's, they will want to rebel simply because they may feel their freedom trampled on. Instead, the teacher can negotiate a short list of rules with their class and this way gives students choice. When students have put together and confirmed their own rules, they will also have a more serious attitude towards them. They will feel more responsible to follow and not break what they had created.

In this context it is also important to recognize the difference between punishment and consequence. If a student was ten minutes late and I gave them twice as much homework as the rest of the class without a previous warning, that would be punishment. I would exercise my power and take away their freedom. However, if we as a class agree that whoever is more than five minutes late either gets more homework or maybe even brings chocolate for the whole group next time to make up for having disturbed everybody, a student arriving late will know very well what to expect - the rules are clear. If somebody is late, getting more homework or buying chocolate would be the consequence, not punishment. Students in this way will know exactly what will happen if they break the rules. They may still choose to do so, but they would expect the agreed consequences.

Fun

A point to think about:
How often do you make the whole class laugh in the sense that they laugh with you and not at you?

Laughter has a great bonding effect and it relaxes the atmosphere in class. Ideally, classes should be entertaining and humorous, although it is sometimes hard to expect so much from the teacher: "The desirability that a teacher be entertaining is a further indication of how difficult it is to be an effective teacher" (Glasser 1998b: 70).

Points to think about:
Think of a good teacher, somebody who had a great influence on you and your teaching. What were their classes like?

Most memorable lessons often happen in classes where teachers manage to combine work with a healthy dose of humour. It is harder to be fond of a teacher who is always serious.

The four needs combined

When Cinderella was sitting at home in despair after her stepmother and the two ugly stepsisters had gone to the ball, she was feeling quite unhappy. The stepmother and her daughters didn't like her; her own father was busy all the time and spent little time with his daughter (no love and belonging). Cinderella dreamed of going to the ball, but was not allowed to. Her own wishes were overlooked, which left her feeling powerless and unimportant (no power). She was not allowed to go to the ball but had to stay at home and work instead. She could not choose what to do that evening (no freedom). The ball was supposed to be an exciting event, while Cinderella was expected to do some chores in the kitchen that evening (no fun).

When her Fairy Godmother appeared, the four-needs situation changed completely. Cinderella remembered that her Godmother loves her and is on her side (love and belonging), by Fairy Godmother's magic Cinderella's wish to go to the ball came true (power). Besides, the prince fell in love with her, which she probably found empowering, too. She probably found the dramatic change of scene quite liberating (freedom), and she had a good time dancing and flirting with the prince at the ball (fun).

Points to think about:
Think about a relationship which is important to you and check if all the four needs are satisfied there. If you notice that you are unhappy about one or more of them, what can you do to change this and get closer to the picture in your quality world?
How do you satisfy the four needs at work? Which need is most successfully covered? Which one isn't?

Now think of your students while still having the four needs in mind. Which of the four needs seems the least satisfied in their situation?

Which of the four needs may disruptive students in your classes need to satisfy the most?

Total behaviour

According to Choice Theory, behaviour in itself is not a simple action or activity, it is a combination of four separate behavioural components and it is therefore called *total behaviour.*

The following "test" will reveal what Glasser means by total behaviour.

Please, follow these instructions:

1. Slow down your heartbeat.
You know you cannot do this, so you most probably haven't even tried.

2. Can you now get angry? Really angry.
You've soon realised that you cannot do this either, at least not directly, because getting angry probably doesn't make sense at the moment. What you need is to think of something to which you usually react with anger and only then can you feel the anger.

3. Think of a monkey. Can you see it in your mind?
You could probably see it for a short time but when you stop reading this, you will forget about it because thinking of a monkey probably doesn't make sense at the moment. However, if you thought you'd lost your car keys, that thought would keep coming back to you because it would make sense for you in that particular situation.

4. Can you close your eyes?

You could probably do this in no time, directly and without hesitation, because you can fully control your actions.

Total behaviour is made up of four components: doing, thinking, feeling and physiology, but despite the fact that all behaviour is chosen, people only have direct control over the first two components, namely doing and thinking. You had no problem closing your eyes just like you don't find it difficult to stand up or stretch or turn around. Thinking, too, is voluntary (unless in dreams) but on one condition – it needs to make sense. The last two components of total behaviour are a bit different, though: when it comes to feeling and physiology, people cannot control them directly. Instead, we can influence them through doing and feeling.

Examples of total behaviour

If I were writing this at work in the computer room with many people around me and somebody there started talking on their mobile phone, I would probably find it disturbing and would get irritated. This would be the *feeling* component of my total behaviour. My blood pressure could go up, which would be the fourth component, *physiology*. I could not change these two components of total behaviour directly, but I could do something on the *doing* and *thinking* levels instead. If I still believed I could influence other people, I could approach the mobile-phone addict and ask them to stop talking in the computer room, or, alternatively, I could simply leave the room for a while, stretch my legs and then come back later. By *doing* something I would also change my *thinking* because when my legs took me out of the irritating situation, I would stop feeling cross. As a consequence of this change, my blood pressure would go down so the change of scene would also indirectly control my *physiology*.

It is important to remember that people always have a choice, even though we can really control only two parts of four-part total behaviour.

Points to think about:

1. *Imagine a situation in class when everything went really well. Think about it for a while and then try to analyse your own total behaviour in that situation.*
What were you doing, thinking and feeling then, and how was your body responding?

2. *Imagine a more unhappy class situation where something went wrong.*
What were the four components of your total behaviour like then?
What were you doing, thinking and feeling, and how was your body responding?

Teachers, disruptive students and total behaviour

According to Choice theory and the way total behaviour works, there is no point in trying to deal with a student who is upset. Being familiar with total behaviour, the teacher can decide not to get drawn into the same behavioural pattern the student has adopted and can - by staying calm - control herself better because she will not focus on her feelings or physiology. Similarly, she will know that if she wants to deal with the situation successfully, she shouldn't focus on the disruptive student's feelings or physiology because the student cannot change those components directly. Instead, the teacher should focus on the student's actions and thoughts.

The worst – and least successful – teacher's reaction in class is to lose their temper. Getting on the *feeling* level of total behaviour will not get anybody anywhere.

There was a science teacher fresh from university, who taught young teenagers. He was enthusiastic about his subject, which is why he tried to elicit answers from his class. Initially, when students did not respond to that with a show of hands and he didn't find himself snowed under with their enthusiastic suggestions, he used criticism. Next time eliciting answers was even less successful, so the teacher added insults to criticism, which later led to a vicious circle. The teacher was getting increasingly disappointed while his students got less and less cooperative.

According to Choice theory, the science teacher broke a couple of basic rules. Firstly, he seemed to be convinced that he could influence students and make them work instead of trying to get them interested in what he was passionate about. Secondly, when his ideal picture of a lesson, the one that was in his quality world, was not met in reality, he allowed himself to react with the pronounced *feeling* component of his total behaviour. In such a state not only did he fail to solve anything, he also brought himself into an emotional state, which was not the best choice in the situation.

What about his students? Naturally, they didn't like being humiliated for days on end, so most of them started hating the teacher *and* his subject. They hated and rejected everything they thought their teacher had in his quality world, above all science itself. In short, students reacted to the teacher's strong *feeling* component by showing their own (negative) feelings.

Teachers who try to coerce students into the kind of behaviour they think is appropriate in a certain teaching situation are not successful in the long run. Glasser and Glasser (1999: 78-79) give the following example of two different approaches to the same problem of a disruptive student. "I'll tell you, John, you're going to have to sit by yourself the rest of the year. Stop bothering everybody around you," mirrors external control, while a Choice theory alternative would go like this: "I'm tired of punishing you, John. I want to be your friend. I think you need some friends. I have time this afternoon during my free period to talk with you about making friends. I'd like to get to know you better." The teacher in the first example could make John sit still for a little while, but the student would soon repeat his behaviour. In the second example, the teacher went beyond the surface, touched on John's psychological needs, especially the possibly unsatisfied need to be loved and to belong, and gave the student choice to actually *do* something about the situation by talking to a calm, understanding adult later that day.

And finally...

Learning is easier if students hold the teacher and her subject in their quality worlds. Teachers get there mostly by establishing a good rapport with students. A teacher who knows the four psychological needs will try to help her students satisfy them in class and will become more a friend to them than a threatening figure of power. Ideally, the teacher should be interested in their students' personal lives and also let them get to know her a little. Glasser (1998: 128) states that teachers often forget how "most students are not on easy personal terms with adults, in many cases not even their own parents". Some teachers feel uneasy about letting students get to know them better, but even sharing some anecdotes from the teacher's life would help students become more supportive of the teacher, because "not knowing another person, especially one who has power over you as a teacher does over a student, makes anyone more likely to cast that person in the role of an adversary or, at least, not as a friend." (Glasser 1998: 129).

When teachers and students appreciate one another, the feeling of caring satisfies the students' need for belonging (or love) while the teachers' readiness to share power, and lead instead of coerce, results in a higher-quality work.

BOOKS

O is a symbol of the world, of oneness and unity. In different cultures it also means the "eye," symbolizing knowledge and insight. We aim to publish books that are accessible, constructive and that challenge accepted opinion, both that of academia and the "moral majority."

Our books are available in all good English language bookstores worldwide. If you don't see the book on the shelves ask the bookstore to order it for you, quoting the ISBN number and title. Alternatively you can order online (all major online retail sites carry our titles) or contact the distributor in the relevant country, listed on the copyright page.

See our website www.o-books.net for a full list of over 500 titles, growing by 100 a year.

And tune in to myspiritradio.com for our book review radio show, hosted by June-Elleni Laine, where you can listen to the authors discussing their books.

mySpirltRadıo